Chicken, Cake and I Do

By

T. R. Cummings

Chicken, Cake and I Do

T.R. Cummings

Published by T.R. Cummings, 2024.

While every precaution has been taken in the preparation of this book, the publisher assumes no responsibility for errors or omissions, or for damages resulting from the use of the information contained herein.

CHICKEN, CAKE AND I DO

First edition. February 20, 2024.

Copyright © 2024 T.R. Cummings.

ISBN: 979-8224821426

Written by T.R. Cummings.

Table of Contents

This book is dedicated to my children. Without you I would have never experienced what unconditional love feels like in this lifetime and for that I am forever grateful. Thank you for allowing me to be your mother.

This book is dedicated to my children.

Without you I would have never experienced what unconditional love feels like in this lifetime and for that I am forever grateful. Thank you for allowing me to be your mother.

That Fateful Morning

Throughout my life I've always has a mental vision of that morning, it's a core memory that I would relive throughout my childhood over and over. Being so young, I never truly grasped what my mind was remembering but as I got older I completely understood what I was seeing during my day dreams that overall simply felt like a nightmare throughout my life. It was a cool summer morning, about 5:30 am. The air was misty with a slight fog as the sunrise revealed fresh dew on the morning grass. The birds were chirping with their usual jubilance and the sun was just beginning to rise in the distance. I distinctly recall sitting in my car seat in the back of the car looking up at the orange Clark sign outside the gas station while wondering what me and my mother were doing there at that time. It was June 2, 1980 and I was just a little over 3 years old. I had no idea what her and I were doing out there so early in the morning, all I knew is that I was with my mom and that I trusted her. So I sat there quietly waiting, looking around and soaking up my surroundings before we headed on to our next destination. We sat there for what seemed like several minutes before she pulled out of the gas station, turned right and traveled the small side road that was about 1000 feet long. The road led up to a large looming campus that sat directly behind the gas station. The main building felt massive and was made out of brick with large white pillars that surrounded the grand entrance. The entire site was sprawling with several smaller adjacent buildings behind the main building. I had never been to this place before and had no idea where we were by the time mom parked the car. I also had no clue that my life was going to be forever altered in this moment. My mother flung her cigarette out the window of our old rusty tan 4 door Ford and stepped out of the car. She came around to my door and helped me get unbuckled and out of the car then took me by the hand and walked me past the towering pillars through the large double wooden doors. She swept me across the shiny marble floor right up to the receptionist whose tiny frame looked like she was being swallowed alive behind the 'large wooden reception counter.

The building itself is beautiful with ornate carvings in the wood and ceilings that seemed like they were as high as the sky. There were large pieces of art hanging on the walls and a small sitting area with some toys and magazines placed on the side tables. In the middle of the room the young woman who sat behind the desk looked up as we walked towards her and asked how she could assist. My mother simply looked at her then down at me and said "I'm here to relinquish custody of her and would like to place her up for adoption". The receptionist compassionately looked at both of us and our unusual predicament and immediately located and notified any available case worker. After a few moments of waiting another young woman appeared from behind the rotunda and as my mother explained to the caseworker her financial and emotional struggles with being a young single mother, the social worker listened to her empathetically and suggested my mother take the time she needed to make necessary improvements on her life and work towards reunifying with me in the future. My mother agreed to enter into a case plan as well as work with the agency to help track down my father, a man whom I had never met while she focused on rebuilding her life. After about an hour of talking to the worker she handed them some of my identifying documentation, some of my favorite toys and several photos of me then looked down at my unsuspecting innocent face, kissed me on the cheek and walked back out the large wooden doors. Leaving me standing there with these unfamiliar people, trying to comprehend in my little three year old mind what was happening to me, and wondering what I had done wrong. From that moment on, I spent the better part of my life searching for the answer to those questions.

I regularly wonder what she did when she got back into her car. Did she take a big sigh of relief? Did she cry? Was she relieved and excited for her future? Did she go home and pick up an article of my small clothing and smell my scent as she wept? Or did she toss all of my toys and clothing into garbage bags and go about her life as if I didn't exist? These questions will probably ruminate in my mind until I take my last breath. And honesty it's probably for the best that I don't know. Because if it turned out to be the latter, I don't know if the three year old inside of me who is still waiting for her mother to return could emotionally handle it. As for me, I was escorted out the back doors to one of the smaller adjacent buildings on the property where the foster children resided. We were separated by our ages in the small cottages and would remain there until a prospective adopter would arrive or simply move cottage to cottage as we got older until we eventually aged out of the system. I remained in that small building for the next 9 days confused, traumatized and waiting for what was to come next, having no idea how that dewy summer morning would impact me for the rest of my life.

Part 1

Lost

Born in 1959 in Akron Ohio, Carol Katherine Murray was the daughter of Irish and French immigrants who made it to America, met, fell in love and settled with their family in Southern Ohio before they eventually migrated to Akron. Carol was the eldest of 4 children growing up in a working class family under the stern alcoholic abusive hand of her father (my grandfather) Joseph Murray. His wife, my grandmother, Mary Louise, was a stay at home mother and homemaker. Although the family enjoyed a fairly comfortable lifestyle due to Joseph's career as a commercial airline pilot, he was a mean abusive drunk who would often take out his rage on his children during one of his blackouts. Along with being an alcoholic, he was openly racist and forbade his children from dating outside their race. By the time Carol was 17 she had endured enough abuse and ran as fast and as far as she could away from the home. She hitchhiked as far as she could and eventually landed in Fort Henryard wood Missouri where she basically just floated through life trying to find her way. With wild strands of red curly hair, penetrating blue eyes and a shapely body that mimicked a soda bottle, she was able to catch the attention of all the boys at the military base. It was also where she caught the eye of Henry Sledge, one of the musicians that played on the base regularly.

Born in 1953, in Hannibal Missouri to Eva Mae Roundtree and Curtis Sledge. Henry Griffin- Sledge spent his childhood hunting, catching fish and playing in caves in the Ozark Mountains. He grew up as an only child under the abusive hand of Curtis Sledge and witnessed his mother be the victim of several domestic violence incidents. Since of both his parents were alcoholics, Henry would try his hardest to steer clear of the home and spent the majority of his childhood inside the idyllic backdrops described in Tom Sawyers Huckleberry Finn novel and was childhood friends with the Lost Boys of Missouri, three young boys who went to explore the caves of Hannibal only never to be seen or heard from again. Town authorities suspect the boys got lost in the caves and perished. Although Henry grew up as an only child he did have an older sister that had been sent to live with a distant family member several years before. Although there was a significant age gap between the siblings, Henry and his sister maintained a familial bond and would remain in regular contact throughout their lives. Despite Henry growing up in difficult circumstances, as he grew older he became an extremely talented musician due to being immersed in musical history growing up. So much so that by the time he was 12 he was traveling nationally with The Temptations as their drummer being touted the youngest band member to ever tour with them. Eva Mae and Curtis operated a road house on the chitin' circuit called the Old Log Cabin that hosted the likes of Ike and Tina Turner and James Brown and as a young child Henry was completely immersed in musical history.

During this time Jim Crow was alive and well and colored artists still weren't permitted to stay in 'Whites only' hotels when they were touring, so they stayed at little juke joints along their tour routes. Several nights Tina Turner was nursed back to health in Henry's bed after one altercation or another with Ike during one of their drunken brawls. Despite the chaos surrounding him, Henry had big dreams of becoming a musician when he grew up so he taught himself to how to play almost every instrument he could get his hands on. From the keyboard to the saxophone, he would stay up all night practicing with whatever band was touring the country and ended up in their home and Ms. Eva Mae kept the door open and the lights on for any traveling artist that needed a warm bed, hot meal and a cold drink. But once Henry turned 18 he had to put his music dreams on hold after he enlisted in the Army where he served for six years and did two tours in Vietnam. Henry spent time traveling the country and eventually ended up back in Missouri playing with his band on the military base.

Not soon after Henry returned to Missouri he met Carol and he was be smitten by charm and looks so they hit it off right away. They dated for several months before the relationship became tumultuous and riddled with alcohol, drugs and allegations of infidelity. After several months together Carol discovered she was pregnant and Henry was hesitant to believe he was the biological father of the child. After numerous attempts at convincing Henry he was in fact the father Carol eventually grew weary of the conversation and resigned herself to the fact that she would be raising this child as a single mother. With basic education, no job, no money and nowhere to live with an infant, she had no choice but to return back to her hometown of Akron with her family while she prepared for the birth of her child. Carol contacted her father Joseph to come pick her up in Missouri and he arrived several days later to retrieve his pregnant, estranged daughter. After a heated exchange between Henry, Joseph and Carol, Joseph finally loaded up his daughter and her meager belongings into his pickup truck and drove the 695 miles back to Akron Ohio.

My journey into this world began on March 28, 1977 in Canton Ohio. Carol had made it back to Akron fairly early on in her second trimester and settled in with her family to prepare for my birth. She began working as a housekeeper and nanny for a local family while attempting to maintain sporadic contact with Henry to no avail. Although she had a normal pregnancy with no major issues, her labor and delivery proved to be problematic. After a long arduous labor and difficult birth, she began hemorrhaging so badly that it almost resulted in her passing away from the severe blood loss. She remained hospitalized in ICU for several days to recover while I was discharged to her family. Her siblings and parents stepped in to care for me as she was kept hospitalized for over a week, denying us those critical moments of bonding after birth. I was only around five lbs.at birth and my complexion was (and still is) extremely light, almost white actually, so when I was born it wasn't evident that I was in fact a black child and I was readily accepted by my grandfather. Since Henry had been questioning my paternity up to this point, with my light skin it almost appeared as if he was correct in his assumptions. But as I got older and my features developed, with thick dark hair kinking up into tight tiny spiral curls and it became evident that I wasn't completely white. Carol recovered shortly after my birth and returned home to care for me, but as I grew older and my features became more pronounced it absolutely infuriated Joseph, and he began make me the focus of his drunken rages while I was just an infant. It soon became clear that I was not safe in the home or to even be left alone with him. Eventually, when Carol had fully healed from the trauma of my birth and was well enough to return to work she managed to scrap together enough money to move her and I into a tiny apartment on the East side of Akron.

I don't recall these years and I only know what I've been told from extended family members and it's probably for the best. The apartment quickly became known as the party house and from the stories I've been told. Carol's drug addiction was beginning to consume her and I was neglected and was sustained on Cheerios and Bologna sandwiches (which I still cannot stomach bologna to this day). On several occasions I was rushed to the hospital due to abuse or neglect with symptoms ranging from severe ear infections to diaper rashes to one hospital report stating that I was being treated for a burn from an iron (Thirty years later I would use these same hospital records to locate and reunite with my biological maternal family). This went on for several months until Carol's addiction took over and she realized she was unable to bear the responsibility of a toddler, herself and a drug addiction. Something had to go, and that something turned out to be me.

Carol attempted to keep it a secret and hadn't told her friends or family of her decision to relinquish me, but as the days passed and they began questioning my whereabouts, she coldly and defiantly stated "I gave her up for adoption", which shocked her friends and infuriated her brother, Joseph Jr. He went on a rampage and physically assaulted her demanding to know where I was and that she return to the agency and retrieve me. When she ultimately refused the entire family stopped speaking to her and by all accounts it was the catalyst that drove the family in separate directions. Joseph and Mary Louise eventually separated and Mary moved her remaining minor children to Texas, leaving only Carol and Joseph in Akron. Later, Joseph would move back to Southern Ohio apparently relieved that his family had left the state never to return and remarried. But despite the turmoil my relinquishment was causing in her family, Carol still believed that it was the best decision she could have made for the both of us. It sure didn't feel that way for me though, all I knew is that I was scared, alone and wanted my mother, regardless of the abuse and neglect I was enduring.

I lived on campus in one of the tiny cottages for nine days before a young white couple entered the grand lobby of the Agency looking to become foster parents. They were high school sweet hearts who were married right out of high school. The man was a welder by trade and the young woman worked part time at a plant store and ran a small childcare business out of her home to make ends meet for their growing family. By the time they walked through the doors of the agency. Over the previous years they had fostered several children and were now ready to adopt a child and provide their young son with a sibling. They went through the rigorous back ground checks and met all of the qualifications and requirements for approval and were excited to continue growing their family through adoption.

I have zero memories of this time frame in my life so all I can do I relay stories I've been told throughout my childhood and the information given to me from my case disposition. One of the stories being that as soon as my adoptive mother entered the room and I laid eyes on her, I reached my arms out for her and cried for her to pick me up. She says that as soon as she had me in her arms she knew she had found her daughter. I went to live with the family as a foster child while still visiting my birth mother over the next 11 months. My case disposition stated that Carol would make half-hearted attempts to improve her life and regain custody of me during this time, but would continually miss visits while appearing on edge and uninterested in bonding or engaging with me when she did make a visit. Within six months' time she had missed six out of fifteen visits and the paperwork states that it appeared to be exceptionally traumatizing for me at the time. My behavior would become extremely aggressive and violent after each missed visit as I would refuse to eat with eating utensils and have extreme outbursts in public. As a 3 year old attempting to understand why her mother had just given her away and why she wasn't coming back-EVER was more than my little mind and heart could comprehend. Time after time I would sit on the Sea Green vinyl couches inside the visitation center, looking at the pastel colored wallpaper and the little bin of toys in the corner and wait to see her appear over the half door with the doorknob that only opened from the outside so that small children couldn't open it and escape.

Despite the agency creating a reunification plan that involved vocational services and counseling, Carol continued to show little to no progress or even interest in getting me back. A little over a full year after she walked through the large wooden doors for the first time, she showed up to our last and final visit bearing pictures of me to present to my adoptive family and was appeared relieved to no longer have the responsibly of caring for me. Throughout the year Carol provided the agency with Henry's name and contact information and that currently she had no way of contacting him. The agency did make several attempts at contacting Henry but all attempts were futile as he was on his own journey of self-destruction at the time.

Once she made the decision to give me away I had no say in the matter. Because nobody cares much about what a 4 year old has to say anyway. It was for the best they said. She was a bad person and on drugs they said. I had a new family now and I should be grateful that they saved me they said. Just be happy is what they told me. But how could I be? I was living with this family who was technically stranger s to me, told this lady I had never met was now my mother and my real mother didn't care about me anymore and to top it off not one of them looked like me in anyway. I was now living with complete strangers. But kids have no say in the matter so in July of 1981, with the stroke of a Judge's pen, Tamara Renee Murray was wiped off the face of the earth and I became Tamara Renee Cummings.

Nobody was coming back for me.

Firestone Park.

Akron, Ohio. In the heart of the city sits a quaint little historic community called Firestone Park. It stand was founded in 1915 by a 22 year old Harvey S. Firestone. Mr. Firestone launched his small tire and Rubber Company with just 17 employees but as the business grew and more workers flocked to this new opportunity, the housing demand increased. The homes in the heart of the Park are all are exceptionally well made colonial brick homes with stunning carvings and wood work inside with beautifully landscaped yards. The streets are lined with lamp posts and dogwood trees that fill the air with a beautiful light fragrance each spring. It's the idyllic backdrop for raising a family or retiring. Looking back I am incredibly thankful to have spent my childhood there.

I would say life was pretty typical in the middle class family I was adopted into. Over the course of seven years my parents would end up adopting three of us and having two biological sons of their own, for a total of five of us. For several years it was my older brother Jason, (who was their biological child and approximately 6 months older than me) and myself although we did always seemed to have a constant stream of foster children. There was Tasha, a curly blond haired blue eyed doll baby of a child that stayed with us for the better part of a year. I can remember playing with her often when I was around five or six. I believe my parents were looking to adopt her as I can recall them being devastated when she was returned to her biological family after living with us for the better part of a year.

Then there was Robbie. He was a little black boy about three or four years old who was terrified of us. The only time he would smile is when my dad would bounce him up and down on his knees while chanting his name in a deep gruff voice. Robbie Robusto is what we would call him and his little face would light up while he screamed with laughter from all the bouncing. What I was told was that Robbie's mother was on drugs when he was removed from her care, but after a while she managed to turn her life around, get sober and regain custody of him. I can also recall my parents crying when he left us because we had built such a strong bond with him and they were worried that he wouldn't be cared for properly.

Then there was Robert who was a twelve year old white kid who wore a colostomy bag. He was the son of a family friend who required long term hospital care due to injuries sustained in a car accident. He didn't come to us through the system, my mom was simply helping a friend. I was about seven when he came to stay with us and I distinctly recall the smell that would emanate from the room when my mom would change his colostomy bag. He lived with us for close to a year and was the last short term foster that my parents accepted

.Between all of the foster kids coming in and out and the children that my mom babysat there was never lack of a playmate as there were usually anywhere between five to seven extra kids running around. They'd range in age from a few months old up to age ten. When I was five years old my mom gave birth to her second biological child, another boy, whom she named Matthew, a dark haired and dark skinned sweetheart of a child who my parents adored. He was a light hearted good natured kid who was extremely intelligent for his age no matter how old he was, the kid seemed to know everything about everything. It was just the three of us for the next two years until my parents decided to adopt again. I don't recall any conversations about them wanting to adopt again, all I know is that one day my mom left and came back with this adorable little girl and said "Say hello to your sister" and that was it.

Now there were four of us.

My little sister Laurie was about 2 when she came and was just a couple months younger then Matthew. She was dark skinned and looked Hawaiian or Indian and she had the cutest little fat cheeks, soft dark curls and deep brown eyes. One of the things that stands out the most after she came to live with us is just a few days after we brought her home and we were all in the garage were fawning over and playing with her. We had just went apple picking the previous day and had several barrels of them stored in the garage for us to snack on and my mom to make apple pies with. Mom was talking on the phone that was attached to the garage wall and the little girl with the curls was just sat there staring at us looking slightly confused at bewildered. It had been reported from the agency that they didn't believe she could walk yet as all she would do is just sit there and stare at people with her dark intense eyes. We sat there on the floor trying to get her to play with us and next thing we knew, that little girl stood up out of nowhere walked over to a barrel of apples, grabbed a juicy red apple and took the biggest bite of one. My mom just looked over at her, chucked and said "Well I guess she can walk" and from that moment on I fell in love with my little sister. She was a very bull headed yet lighthearted child and still has the same demeanor as an adult. Sister and I spent quite a bit of our childhood having singing contests in our bedroom to determine who the better singer was. She totally was but I'll never tell her that.

It was just the four of us for a few years until one day we came home from school and there were two random white kids at our kitchen table devouring any and every morsel of food they could get their hands on. We were taken aback at their condition because they couldn't talk very well despite being four and five years of age as they were developmentally delayed from the abuse and neglect they experienced. Patrick was a five year old blonde haired blue eyed boy with a cowlick in the front of his hair and his little sister Melissa, who was four, had brown hair brown eyes and exact same cowlick in the exact same place as her brother. At first we weren't sure what to make of these kids as they always seemed to be hungry and no matter how much they ate they were never satisfied. Patrick could eat plates that would fill a grown man and still be asking for more food and at times we would catch them eating out of the trashcans because that's what they were accustomed to. They both remained with us for about 9 month and occasionally visited with their birth parents until one day their extended biological family stepped in and decided to adopt them both. My parents told us that although they wouldn't be going back home they would be going to live with their aunt and uncle and cousins. Patrick and Melissa were pretty excited to be going back to live with their family in some capacity and helped my parents pack their belongings into their bags and get them into the back of the long station wagon. Mom and Dad loaded us all up in the car and we went as a family to say our goodbyes when we dropped them off. But once we arrived at the family's home, the woman of the house pulled my parents to the side and quietly informed them that had a change of heart and that they would only be adopting the little girl. After she walked away my parents stood in the driveway shocked and saddened while trying to explain to my little brother why his sister was staying there and he couldn't and that he had to come back and live with us while she lived there. The last memory I have of her is of us pulling out of the driveway waving goodbye to her as she stood in the large bay window waving back. Patrick not only lost his parents due to their inability to provide a stable home, but in a cruel twist of fate he also lost his little sister. It was heartbreaking, and I'll never understand why they did something so selfish and cruel to those children. He never saw her again after that.

But despite all of our hardships, to the outsider it would appear that life was good in our little corner of the world. My parents worked hard to give us as many opportunities as they could and proved us with a home that we probably wouldn't have had otherwise. We lived in a 3 story home in the middle of "The Park" as it was referred to by us long timers. We had an above ground pool in the backyard, bikes, toys a pool table in the garage and a basketball hoop. My dad installed the hoop after he black topped the driveway for us to be able to roller skate on. My mom would clean my dance instructors home every Saturday morning in order to get my dance classes at a discount. I danced tap jazz and ballet in my early childhood, then went on to play Tennis, Softball and Basketball in my later years. My dad would spend hours teaching me how to actually hit the ball with the bat without closing my eyes when the I would see the ball coming and my mom always had her camcorder out and recording at all of my dance recitals. Despite all of the ways we presented as a normal family, I just couldn't shake the feeling of not belonging or that I was never good enough. These feelings would plague me throughout my life and I can recall the first time I experienced them as a child. My brother and I were both little over four years old and he had just started preschool at a local church. My mom he and I would walk down there every day to drop him off while he excitedly told me about his friends. Every day I would watch him run in the door and start playing with them immediately, grabbing toys and riding bikes in the parking lot, while I stood back wondering why I couldn't go in as well. If I recall right my mom told me it was because I wasn't old enough but it didn't matter to a four year old child. All I knew is that he was getting special treatment while I walked back to the house with mom and waited for hours for him to return and tell me about his day. I wanted to be a part of something as well, and to fit in and have friends, but day after day I got to watch him get dropped off and go inside while I remained back wondering why. As an adult with children, I completely understand the whole age situation, but as a little girl who was now alone and having to carve out her own place in this world, it left me feeling dejected and not good enough.

We always had an array of dogs, cats, birds, fish, and hamsters in the house while growing up. I can recall this one time when I was about nine, mom had gotten us sibling lizards. We were so excited because they were Chameleons and we'd watch them for hours waiting to see if they would change colors. Part of my responsibilities was to clean their tank out with the hose on the side of the house. I pulled out one of the lizards and as I was cleaning the tank and held it by its tail. For whatever reason, I began to swing it around. To my utter horror I watched as the lizard went flying across the yard. But when I looked down at my hand I was still holding its tail. It was still twisting around in my hand as I asked myself "What have I done, have I killed this poor thing?" Then almost simultaneously thought to myself "Why is this things tail still moving"? I was so worried that I killed it, and honestly may have, because to this day I have no idea if we ever recovered that lizard or not.

Our summers consisted of annual vacations to Myrtle Beach at my grandmother's trailer by the ocean, camping, and trips to Geauga Lake. We would go camping in Loudonville a couple times a year and spend our summers canoeing or rafting down the Mohican River and hunting for crawfish and tadpoles. Mom would come out to the river with us occasionally but most of the time she would be back at the campground cooking, leaving us to roam and explore the world around us with each other. It was a wonderful way to spend a childhood. Everything was cooked over the fire, and it was delicious. Mom would always bring a loaf of Wonder bread and cherry or apple pie filling to make these little pocket pies for dessert. We'd put the bread into this little pie maker with a long handle, add the filling and hold it over the fire. After dinner and walking up to the showers, we'd spend our nights around the fire laughing and popping popcorn. At bedtime we all would pile into our little pop up camper listening to the other campers in the distance and crickets chirping, while smelling the burning embers from nearby camp sites.

On weekends you could usually find us at one family member's house or another. Both of my parents came from large families, so there was always a cousin or two around to play with. All of my extended family members on both sides were Caucasian. Literally everybody except me. I can't say growing up I recall anyone treating me differently from anyone else in the family except for that one openly racist uncle. When we were younger we would play with cousins on both sides of our family but as we got older around age 10-11 we didn't see much of our family on my mother's side, until one day we didn't see them at all anymore. She also forbade us to speak to any of them again. To this day I still have no clue as to what occurred that caused her to cut off her entire family all at one time, but I still have managed to keep in contact with one of my cousins from that side over the years.

Due to her in-home childcare she was able to be a stay at home mother and still earn a living, giving us the typical middle class life at that time. Dad would come home from work to a hot, home cooked, unseasoned meal and a clean house and would spend his free time drinking a beer or two watching football while working on his model cars and airplanes with his twin brother, my Uncle Tim. His work space always smelled of Tester's model glue and acrylic paint and he'd spend hours upon hours making them things while listening to Moody Blues or Crystal Gayle on his record player in his study. To this day he has hundreds of them models that he's made and still keeps them displayed around his workshop on shelves and hanging from the ceilings. Mom was a superb seamstress and our dining room table always seemed to be piled high full of reams of fabric and different crafting projects. It used to be piled so high that it would take an entire day for all of us to clean it off for Thanksgiving dinner only for it to be piled high again by the very next night.

Although I have very few memories of my mom's side of the family and probably couldn't pick one of them out of a line up, Dad's side of the family was completely different. He came from a large, close knit, loud, part Hungarian family. He had his twin brother and three sisters, and they each had children. There was 13 cousins in total and they accepted all of us adopted children with open arms. I have very fond memories of family gatherings, holidays, and spending time at our grandparents home. We'd spend hours playing in our grandparent's large back yard with our cousins doing everything from eating the bitter purple grapes that grew on the vines, coloring in the activity books she kept for us or tossing these three sided disks Grandma kept around. I never really knew and still have no clue, what them disks were really for or what we were supposed to do with them, besides playing weird games of fetch with each other there wasn't much else to use them for. Grandma always had Verner's ginger ale and root beer floats on deck and I can still recall the distinct taste of the well water at their home and seeing the iconic picture 'Grace' hanging above their sofa. Grandpa, a loud bolstering WWII vet would playfully grab my face and rub his rough beard stubble across it. It felt so rough on my skin and used to tick me off because it kind of hurt. He would also tease me and tell me if I kept eating cucumbers that one day a plant would grow inside my stomach and I actually believed him for a couple years.

Of all my extended family, I carried a special affinity for my dad's eldest sister, my Aunt Judy, but we'll get to her later in the story.

Childhood

Although my adopted family tried to give me the best life they could, I still I spent most of my childhood searching for my place in this world. I was shamed for being adopted and my adopted mother, although she was an absolute saint for adopting me and not allowing me to experience the traumas that can come with growing up in the foster system, she simply was not one of them loving kind mothers that could help us work through the complicated traumatic emotions of being adopted. Her response was more like "yep your biological parents were pieces of shit and on drugs so they gave you up for adoption so deal with it". There was never any affection or loving words of affirmation, she just remained very cold and sterile about the whole situation. And as much as they tried to provide me with as much normalcy as possible, life just felt unbearable at times. No matter how many kids were around it just seemed scary lonely and confusing and I in the back of my mind I was constantly worrying that I would do something wrong again and have to go live with another family. I felt disposable to say the least. Growing up I didn't have many friends at all as I was too white for the black kids (plus I never seen any in our neighborhood) and I was too black for the white girls. I was a skinny super light (even pale at times) clumsy kid with a big poof of dry broken nappy and distressed hair. My adoptive mother had no clue how to maintain colored kinky hair. Her solution was VO5 hair dressing which did nothing but leave my hair looking like a matted steel wool poof on my head resulting in me being called 'brillo pad' while growing up. In middle school she tried to feather the sides and cut bangs since it was a popular hair style among my white schoolmates at that time. But with dry crunchy hair, it looked like a multi-dimensional afro.

The front around the edges short and the back long. A mullet perhaps. A steel wool mullet but mom said it looked 'nice'. But With my lack of style and constant hair crisis, I was the target of severe bullying. I never felt as though I was able to fit in and it always left me feeling lost, out of place and in search of something. On top of looking awkward, I always felt insecure and out of place. I was dubbed a "weirdo" by my classmates at an early age and as I grew up I just couldn't shake it. The more I tried to not be "normal" the more awkward I became and I just didn't fit in anywhere.

When I was about five, we were visiting an extended family member's farm. I believe she was an aunt on my dad's side and her name was Ethel Mae. She had cows, horses, chickens and goats. My brother Jason and I would chase each other through the barn and under the animals for hours. In the winter you could find me in my red snowsuit and my brother Jason in his blue snowsuit running around and squealing with delight exploring the old barn and all of the animals. One day while playing hide and seek and darting in and out underneath the animals usual, I happened to stop right underneath a cow. Being five years old I was still pretty short and was going to use it to my advantage and figured he would never find me hiding beneath a cows tail. As I'm standing there waiting to be found I hear a voice in the distance shouting "Oh Tammy! Please move away from the cow, she just had a baby!" I was clueless as to what they meant so I continued to just stand there. Everyone kept shouting at me that the cow just had a baby and I was so confused on why they were so frantic so I looked up to see if there was a baby cow somewhere hiding too, and in the exact moment that I looked up, the cow released its bowels. I was completely covered, but for the sake of all of our stomachs here I'll spare you the gory details. But I will tell you that the feces was not solid and I had to be hosed off in the barn before I could ride back home in the car and I don't recall ever going back to Aunt Ethel Mae's farm again after that day.

My awkwardness and lack of grace continued as I got older and I would experience some the most absurd and asinine injuries from sheer clumsiness. Some of them were self-inflicted and some of them not. Such as the time I was coming down a slide in the first grade and a wood chip from the playground flew up and landed in my eye. I remember being seen at the hospital the doctor using some type of spinning drill type of tool to extract the wood chip. That injury resulted in me having to wear an eyepatch for a week and my mom having to apply an ointment to my eyeball for a week afterwards to prevent infection. Then, that same year, I tried jumping off a swing for the first time mid swing, but I didn't know I had to wait until the swing swung forward to jump so as I swung backwards I jumped off and landed flat on my face in front of my entire class. . Thankfully I didn't need medical attention for that one. Then a few years later, in the fourth grade I was sitting at my desk in class and a classmate was walking past me carrying a piece of paper. Somehow, as she walked past the paper came in contact with my eye and I ended up with a paper cut on that same eye so I was back to the eye patch and antibiotic eye goop for a week. Luckily my eye wasn't permanently damaged from either incident.

Despite our large family, mom always tried to ensure we felt special on our birthdays. It was 1987, I had just turned ten and Michael Jackson's thriller album had just come out. Like many other girls my age I was completely in love and obsessed with him. The months leading up to the party my mom worked hard on sewing a replica of the costume that Michael had worn on the Billie Jean album cover, down to the gloved hand. She had arranged for my little brother Matthew to wear the outfit as he jumped out of a large box to surprise me at my birthday part that year. My dad brought out his large record player and speakers and we blasted the album throughout the night as my friends and I danced and ran around the back yard and playing on our swing sets. We had two of them in the yard and one had swings while the other had monkey bars and a slide. .Once again I attempted to wow my guests how agile I was by jumping from one swing set to another in a feeble attempt to further impress them. I climbed up the large A-frame set with the swings and leapt through the air reaching for the monkey bars on the other set that was just a few feet way. But instead of grabbing the bars I completely missed and somehow managed to rip open the skin on my chest from a rusty bolt that was sticking out. My mom frantically called all my friends parents to come pick them up and raced me to the Emergency room. Somehow, thankfully I didn't need stiches and was bandaged up and given a tetanus shot. My parents spent the next several days forcing me to cross the monkey bars multiple times a day so that my arm wouldn't get tight from the tetanus shot. For years after that incident I had a scar running from the top left of my chest to the bottom right.

The next time I had friends over was for a skating party was the 5th grade. The year was 1988 and Tone Loc's Wild Thang had just come out. I grew up listening to classic rock, and was just hearing hip hop music for the first time at this age. I mean, sure we listened to Michael Jackson and Prince, but groups like Run DMC and 2 Live Crew were unheard of in our home. We've got the Tone Loc playing in the garage on my little purple cassette player and my friends and I were skating and just having a great time. We still had the same two A-frame swing sets in the back yard with the swings, slides and monkey bars on them Since the larger swing set only had swings on it, it made the perfect tent with just a couple of sheets hung over the top bar. After tiring out from skating, my friends and I were in our 'tent' playing games of tag and hide and go seek. I was so excited at the idea of having friends over that I was running back and forth between the 2 'tents' making sure everyone was having a good time. On one specific pass through I didn't duck low enough and I ran full force towards the exit and smacked the middle of my forehead on one of the cross bars of the swing set. My head immediately began pounding and my ears started ringing and I just laid there in shock. Mom came out concerned and pissed at the same time. She sent everyone home and kept an eye on me for the night to make sure I didn't need to be seen in the Emergency room- yet again. .

Of all the stories my adoptive parents or I could tell you about me, there's one specific incident that has become infamous in my family and to this day still causes my dad to laugh until tears stream down his face. A little background on this story is that my brothers always played soccer when I was growing up. I would sit on the sidelines and watch their moves and think "that's so easy, I could do that". But the fear of being kicked in the shins prevented me from ever actually playing.

I was in the 5th grade and I was coming out school through the back parking lot where I knew my dad would be waiting to pick me up. He had one of them old Chevy vans it was a light faded green and white and was covered in Bondo. Even though playground and parking lot were separated by a fence, they were close enough that as I walked out I could see him looking at me through the van window. The entire school was outside Out of the corner of my eye I could see classmate rolling a ball across the parking lot. As I walked towards my dad's van I noticed the ball coming right towards me. It was a round black ball. In my mind all I could think was "This is it Tamara, go kick that ball and show them how good you are at soccer, they're definitely going to think you're cool now." So I ran. I ran full speed towards that ball, pulled my leg back and kicked it as hard as I could. Only the ball didn't move. The ball just stopped and stayed there. And me? I landed flat on my face on the concrete. This ball was not a soccer ball or any other type of ball you could kick for any reason. It was a 12 lb. bowling ball.

As I awkwardly picked myself up off the ground and continued walking towards my dad's van, I was mortified. And now bearing scraped up knees and hands, I opened the heavy van door to climb inside, only to be greeted by him with tears pouring g down his cheeks. He was laughing so uncontrollably hard that he was crying literal streams of tears. The more he wiped his eyes and tried to stop laughing the more he would start crying and laughing all over again. This went on for about 15 minutes while I sat there crest fallen and nursing my wounds. I waited for him to compose himself enough to drive the 5 blocks back to our house. To this day, over 30 years later, he still cries actual tears when he recalls that story.

It would be an absolute lie to say my adoptive family gave me a terrible childhood. There was a lot of love in the home I grew up in. A lot of wonderful memories. As I grew older, I grew more confused, and felt misplaced and out of place, so I began to act out. I became interested in sex at very early age for no particular reason. I can recall experimenting with a little girl my mom was babysitting. We were both about seven years old and we performed oral sex on each other behind my bedroom door. My mom found us and burst in demanding answers and the best answer I could come up with was Hide and Seek. It sounded perfectly reasonable to my juvenile mind at that time. That is, until my mom aggressively shouted "Hide and go seek? In the dark? With your clothes off?" I realized as she was saying it how absolutely absurd it sounded but I was already locked in and couldn't go back now. So yes mom, we like playing hide and seek butt naked in the dark in the middle of the day on a Tuesday. That wasn't the worst part though, because we all know that seven year olds aren't known for the best hygiene practices and frankly they don't wipe good. I'll never forget how it tasted like pee and I immediately knew back then that I never wanted to taste that again. I'm absolutely positive that that single episode prevented me from becoming bisexual or gay. Now, don't get it twisted, I love my gays. Any or shape or color or size gays I'll take. But for me it's just not worth the risk again. Urine in my mouth once was enough for me to learn my lesson. I was also a bed humper. And boy did I used to hump that mattress to death. But in a home with 4 other siblings, parents and a slew of other kids I had to get creative and learn how to move swiftly bet we're not going to take about all that.

I was just a bed humping nappy headed little weirdo.

The year was 1988 and I was in the 5ᵗʰ grade. That year we had all just horrifically witnessed the Challenger explosion live on television during class but I don't think any of us truly understood the magnitude and trauma of witnessing that horrendous event. . My teacher that year was an older white man whose family owned a popular pizza shop in North Akron so he would occasionally surprise us with pizza chicken and jo-jo's and I can recall him bringing in several peperoni pizzas in the large white boxes for us as we watched history horrifically unfold.

Not only was I having a difficult time fitting in with my peers, I was also singled out by the teachers, him being one of them. At this age my friends were all starting to wear makeup, and finding their style. Cute oversized overalls, Hammer pants, big colorful block clothing, and leg warmers were just some of the styles. I would over hear the girls talking about sharing clothes and going to the malls to go shopping while I was barely allowed to leave our block let alone go to the mall and shop, so naturally I didn't have any of that type of clothing in my closet. Maybe some leg warmers from when I did ballet but that's about it because mom would dress me in paisley gauchos, thrifting finds and handmade garments. When I asked her for a t-shirt of my favorite band New Kids on the Block, she said the shirts cost too much and we could make our own. And that's what we did.

She packed up into her old station wagon and we headed to the local craft store where we purchased some plain neon green, yellow and orange t-shirts along with some black puff paint. That night we sat at the kitchen table and with the black puff paint wrote 'New Kids on the Block' on all of my new neon shirts. The letters were written in a 5ᵗʰ grade penmanship and came out sloppy, crooked and written on a slant, but my mom insisted they "looked nice, and that was the style" and for some reason I believed her. Even though I hadn't seen a single other person wearing these puff painted neon shirts I tried to make them work. I just wanted something to help me fit in, just a little bit. I attempted to doctor up the look the best way I could with what I had on hand at home. Some leggings and a black belt, along with my bright blue eyeliner and some tangerine lip balm to top off the look. My mom had gotten me these zip on shoes for school and you could interchange the tops of the shoes to different styles and colors and with a quick zip. I had several patterns to choose from but one day the zipper got stuck on the bright yellow shoe top so now I could only wear yellow shoes because I couldn't get them unzipped to change them to a different pattern. The next morning I got dressed in my new puff paint shirt, rimmed my upper and lower lid in blue eyeliner threw on my yellow shoes and with a quick spritz of my Exclamation! Perfume I headed to school. I walked through the classroom doors feeling pretty confident and feeling like just this one time I might actually be able to fit it only to hear my teacher exclaim "What happened to you"?

The entire class got quiet and froze while I silently prayed that it was me he was talking to but I looked up only to see him looking directly at me. As I stared back at him I could feel my stomach sinking and was trying figure out a way to crawl into myself without anyone noticing me disappearing. He repeated in front of the entire class "You look like you have blue fungus on your eyes and bananas on your feet"! The whole class erupted while I stood there mortified and embarrassed. I spent the rest of the day feeling like a complete clown in my homemade concert shirt and moldy looking eyelids. My hair had pretty much taken on the shape of a helmet by this point completely dry fried and brittle. It literally didn't move. It was just a big dry poof in the shape of a helmet and I looked a mess. I wanted the long pretty curly hair the other mixed girls had. I wanted to feel my hair sweep across my face when the wind blew. I wanted to know what it felt like to have cute clothes and feel pretty. I wanted to know what it felt like to have a real mom and dad who looked like you. I wanted to know what it felt like to have a real family with a place to belong

Middle school was more of the same of trying to fit in and make friends. At this point my friends were having regular sleep overs on the weekends and school nights while I wasn't allowed out past 7pm and my bedtime was at

9pm sharp. The idea of a sleepover on a school night was absolutely wild and unheard of to me and I couldn't believe they were so lucky to have such cool parents! While they were having parties I was busy watching episodes of Full House and The Fresh Prince. It was in middle school is when I also noticed how many other black kids were around because I never seen them outside of school or anywhere at the parks. A block up from our house there was a street called Archwood, and growing up we were forbidden to ride or bikes or cross over that street into to that side of the neighborhood. We didn't question it much as Archwood was a fairly busy road so we assumed it was for our own safety. Later I realized that all of my black classmates lived over there and they rarely if ever crossed over the street to play at the park or at any of our houses. All of the friends I ever played with while growing up were white. Firestone Park has an unspoken rule for the families that live across Archwood that they aren't welcome on the other side of the street or in the Park. The only reason I am aware of it is because throughout my life I've lived on both sides of Archwood and the quality of life is drastically different. Needless to say I lived a fairly sheltered life that didn't involve hip hop music, parties with my friends or even seasonings. I didn't even know fried chicken existed until I ran away a couple years later. Up until that point I had only eaten chicken legs that were coated in Shake n bake. They were always burnt on the bottom and tasted awful but I didn't know any better so I ate it. I had no idea what cabbage, greens, wings, dressing, or even what soul food was for that matter. And I definitely didn't know ya'll were putting meat in your spaghetti. I was literally getting sauce and noodles. I guess from the outside looking in life seemed pretty normal and bland, but then one day tragedy struck and everything changed.

Aunt Judy

My beloved aunt Judy (dad's sister) was a large hearty woman with thick jet black poufy hair, olive skin and lavender glasses. She and her husband, Uncle Mike had 5 children. Pat, Allen, Warren, Marie and Julie Aunt Judy wore her smile like a badge and always had a snappy witty comeback. She smoked cigarettes like a chimney and drank coffee all day long. She worked as a waitress at a local diner called Lou and Hyde's and everybody loved her. Her spirited laugh and bubbling personally attracted many colorful friends. Of all my family I can say she was the person who I felt understood me the most. She lived in a multi-cultured neighborhood on the West side of Akron in a well-worn house on a dead end street. I distinctly remember she had a stair case that you could go up from the living room, cross the landing then go back down into the kitchen. It was the coolest thing for a kid. Her door, heart and arms were always open no matter what her own personal struggles were. We shared a beautiful bond and she was one of the only people I felt I could trust. I remember her telling me when I was 12, "Tammy never marry a man for love. Always marry him for money. The love can come later". Aunt Judy was funny honest and strong and I always felt a deep connection with her. She radiated and a love that felt real and pure with no strings attached to it.

As I opened my eyes one spring morning in 1992, right before my 15th birthday, my mother appeared in my bedroom doorway with red puffy eyes. The kind where you can tell the person has been crying for hours. She looked at me and simply said "Your Aunt Judy died last night" and walked back out. I sat there in shock. I couldn't understand, she had been perfectly fine the previous weekend when we visited her but after suddenly falling ill and ending up in the hospital the doctors said a blood clot traveled to her lungs and caused her death. I was devastated. At the age of 13, I had never felt so consumed by grief. The day of her funeral, I walked up to her casket to say my goodbye and almost collapsed right there. My dad managed to catch me just before I hit the floor. Her passing rocked the entire family to the core and things never the same again. There became less and less gatherings until one day we just didn't have them at all anymore. We would still see our cousins, but very rarely all together.

I truly believe her death was the ultimate catalyst that caused my life to take the turn that it did shortly thereafter. It's also when Trichotillomania emerged its ugly head and I started pulling my hair out. By the time I got to her funeral I had managed to pull all of my eyebrows out. I also had no idea at that time how this disorder would come to control my life and destroy my self-confidence as I grew older.

I was finishing my 9th grade year in the fall after Aunt Judy passed. Each day became an excruciating battle to try to act as un-weird as possible trying to fit in but no matter what I did it felt like I just couldn't win with these kids and moving into high school only broadened the scope of bullying. Before it was just kids teasing kids, now it seemed the peer pressure was way more intense in extremely different ways and my desire to belong reached a whole new level. The nicknames also began to evolve as I went from being called Brillo pad in grade school to being called Q tip (because I was skinny with a poufy top) and mosquito bites (because of my flat chest) in middle school only to be accused of stuffing my bra when I finally did blossom in high school. I was nothing like the other kids. I didn't have the cool clothes, or get invited to the cool parties and even if I was invited it was either a prank or I wouldn't be allowed to go. That fall one of my classmates had a party and I was actually invited and allowed to go. She told me it was a costume party and that everyone would be dressed up. Something in my gut told me this was some type of set up, so I decided to wear my Poison t-shirt and would just say I was a punk rocker in case I was the only one not in some type of full costume. Sure enough, I pull up to the party and everyone is standing there wide eyed and mouths open in anticipation. Not a single person was wearing a costume. Kids can be real dicks man.

Because I was so naïve and looking for acceptance I was an easy target for the older kids in school, especially the boys and because I was not used to any type of male attention I relished in it. They weren't really doing any to make me feel special or wanted, they were simply just noticing me. I was blossoming and developed a very naturally curvy physique and that was also attracting quite a bit of attention that I absolutely wasn't used to. Now the older boys were commenting on my breasts or tiny waist and I finally felt like I was finally being seen. But the attention quickly turned negative when it was revealed that I was still a virgin. The nicknames continued to evolve and eventually by the middle of my 9th grade year, I went from the weirdo to the big V to the big hoe. I'm not exactly sure how it got out that I was a virgin but I probably mentioned it in passing with a friend. It felt like the entire school knew and was shocked that I hadn't had sex yet and it seemed like I some sort of failure and was yet again, behind the other girls and not able to keep up. While they were buying bras and I was flat as a board, while most of them had begun their menstrual cycles I was trying to decide if the fake cramps I was experiencing were from pre or post menstruation when asked. They were going to parties and concerts while I was looking forward to the next episode of America's funniest home videos that was televised on Saturday nights. So when I found out my friends were having sex too I really felt like I was behind the rest of the kids! Not behind in a developmental manner but more of in a way that these kids were all doing and experiencing things and I none of this was happening in my life. I just wanted to fit in and have some type of similarity. So when word got out that I was still a virgin the following day at school I was dubbed "The big V". I was being made fun of for still being a virgin. You could hear kids from all grades yelling it up and down the halls when I walked by, it was so embarrassing and I thought I was literally the only kid in the school that was still a virgin. So I decided I was going to show them that I wasn't this big virgin they spoke of and I was going to have sex.

Somehow.

There was this older boy in the 11th grade that I had a crush on. He was black kid but burn out and a bad boy and I really wanted him to notice me. I started hanging out at a neighborhood hangout that he basically lived at and struck up a friendship with his best friend's sister so I'd have a reason to continually be at the house. Within about a week of hanging out there I found myself behind a dirty blanket that was used to partition off a section of the basement that he used as his bedroom. I was wearing a black shirt, some black and white polka dot gaucho shorts and some yellow panties. We climbed into his bed and he kissed me. I could taste the cigarettes on his lips. It didn't taste disgusting but it was very distinct, enough that to this day when I kiss someone who smokes I'm immediately taken back to that moment. We didn't have any foreplay and he just plopped it in. I wasn't expecting the pain to be so intense. I had never been taught anything about sex or how the female body worked so I didn't know what to expect. Once it was over he got off me and I pulled my panties up. We laid there talking for a while and he decided he wanted round 2. I had no idea my hymen was broken or that there was going to be blood involved, so when I looked down as I pulled my panties down I was mortified to see the blood but didn't dare say anything to him and just prayed he didn't notice. Just as we were finishing up one of his friends came downstairs, pulled the curtain back and shouted "Oh my god dude! She's got blood on her panties!!" I pulled my pants up and raced the 6 blocks back home. By the time I got home the blood had leaked though my panties and onto my white shorts. Thankfully my mom wasn't around when I ran upstairs to change and hide my clothing and soaked the shorts in cold water.

When I returned to school the next day my nickname had been changed. Formerly known as 'The big V', I was now dubbed "The big Hoe". So now when I walked the halls that's what you'd hear shouted out. The Big Hoe.

Basketball season had just kicked off and we were having a pep rally to celebrate the teams. I had tried out and made the girls team and have no idea how. They must have been short on recruits that year because I was an absolutely terrible basketball player. I made one basket the entire season and it was on accident, I threw the ball and ran away and when I looked back it actually went into the basket. During the pep rally, my team and I stood on the gymnasium floor waiting our turn to step forward and have our name and position be announced. The entire school was cheering and dancing and energized. As each person's name was called and they got closer to me I began to feel extremely nervous. They called my name and I stepped forward. But the cheering stopped. I stood there staring into the crowd when a slow roar began to sound. At first I couldn't make out what they were saying, but as it got louder and more people joined, in it became clear what they were shouting. The word Hoe. Long, loud, drawn-out. Just the word HOOOEEEEEEE rippling through the audience. I was mortified and embarrassed to say the least. In some ways I've spent my entire life trying to outrun that experience and that word.

By winter of my freshman year my reputation was getting around to other schools. A classmate's brother at another local school had heard about me and asked her if she knew me. I had never interacted with this particular girl until the day she invited me over for a 'sleep over" she said her brother thought I was cute and wanted me to come over and hang out. He was 17 and a senior at a rival high school. After concocting a plan with my best friend that I would be at her house lying to my parents about my whereabouts, I was off to spend the night with my new friend. We started off the night drinking Mad Dog 2020 in their basement. It was a finished basement with a sitting area that consisted of old couches and chairs. It was me, her, her brother Jason, and 3 of his friends. It was my first time ever drinking alcohol outside of a swipe or 2 of dad's beer when he wasn't looking. We sat around drinking and laughing for several hours before Jason started making sexual advances and passes at me. I'm sure I would have been an easy target without being in my inebriated state and I don't recall at what point I succumbed to his advances or how the actual act of sex began, but I do recall that it was completely pitch black and I couldn't see who was on top of me. But I could feel the bodies changing shape periodically and I began to realize that I was having sex with multiple people. But in the dank dark basement I could not see a single face. I could tell when it was Jason as he was extremely heavy and I began shouting "get off me" because with his weight it felt like there was a building on top of me. At one point during the assault and he placed his hand over my mouth while instructing me to "shut the fuck up" because his grandma was upstairs and would hear my cries for help.

After they were finished, I left the house that night carrying a trauma that would follow me for decades. I didn't dare tell my mom because I had lied about my whereabouts I and didn't want to get into trouble. I didn't tell my closest friends because I thought it was my fault and with my reputation nobody was going to believe me anyway. This is the first time I'm speaking about it publicly as it has haunted me for many years believing this was somehow my fault. And maybe it was for putting myself in that situation. But with nobody to talk to about it with or tools to process it I would journal about it in my diary about it while blaming myself for what had happened to me that night. I never spoke to my classmate again after that night and went about my life pretending it never happened.

My little colorful Lisa Frank diary with the tiny padlock on it knew all of my secrets and my fears and I would write them down, lock it away and know that everything was secret and safe with Lisa. That was, until the day my mom found it, broke it open and read everything. Every single one of my secrets. The day she found it and read it she picked me up from school which was out of the ordinary because mom never picked us up and she took me to McDonalds, which was another extreme rarity. We talked about what she had found and she informed me that she was going to have to tell my dad and I was grounded indefinitely. She never once discussed with me the importance of safe sex, or my reasoning as to why I felt like I needed to use sex as a means to feel loved or the possibility of teenage pregnancy. She told me to stop having sex, gave diary back to me and grounded me. I assumed since she now knew all my secrets that I was safe to continue writing in it but not even 2 weeks later I come home from school to find her holding it in her hands again. She had now highlighted the parts about my sexual activity in bright yellow. Since I was grounded at home and couldn't leave the house I began flicking school to meet with boys and 1 time I actually had sex at school in one of the trade shops (I think it was the auto body shop). Being 14 I didn't know the pleasures of sex, I only knew these boys liked me and I was looking for any affection I could get my hands on. Between the sex I was actually having and the rumors about me giving head in the bleachers (if you're a classmate from high school and reading this I want you to know that absolutely did NOT happen) I probably had the worst reputation in the school and I can only imagine the embarrassment my brother endured having me as a sister.

Once again she gave my diary back and this time tore it to pieces because my secrets or fears weren't safe anywhere. I threw the little torn highlighted shreds of paper in my trashcan and left them there. I went to school the next day as usual only to come home and again find my diary sitting on the table as she had painstakingly taped each piece back together with scotch tape. But this time she didn't give it back to me, she called some of my Aunts and Uncles over for dinner and they sat around the table reading and passing it around while discussing what I had written. Together they decided that I needed therapy so my mom scheduled me an intake appointment at Child Guidance. Although I was reluctant to go, I was hopeful for the chance to have someone to confide in. This was before HIPPA laws were in affect so all my mother had to do was call the therapist and ask them questions about how my sessions were going and what I talked about. I attended therapy for about 3 weeks before my mom began questioning me about what I had told my counselor and me sugar coated and downplayed what I had been discussing. But once she spoke with the counselor she became enraged at what I had told them and I was whopped and grounded for it. After that I refused to talk to the counselor or anyone else for that matter because I just couldn't trust ANYONE, and the one person who I could trust was now dead.

Meeting Morgan

Being young, vulnerable and broken while on my ongoing search for love eventually led me into the arms of an older man. I met him right after Aunt Judy passed as I was ending my 9th grade year right and hadn't turned 15 just yet. This black guy had been hanging around the neighborhood and I come across him while playing catch football with some neighborhood kids that he was also friends with. He seemed nice enough but he was older than me by 9 years making him 23 years old to be exact. Once he approached me to hang out and showering me with complements, it felt like he was giving me the acceptance and validation and I was so desperate for. I quickly became enamored by the attention he lavished on me and finally felt seen and accepted but my parents quickly found out his age and forbade me to continue seeing him. But the more they pulled the more I pushed and it became quite contentious around the house. Eventually I would begin sneaking out at night to see him and when I got caught I'd simply run away. One late night when I was returning home I found my dad sitting on the couch waiting for me. He was furious and boy did he whoop my tail but that didn't stop me. I would put scotch tape on the doors when I snuck out at night so I could tell if someone had opened it before I would attempt to reenter the house. Time and time again I would get caught, taken to the Detention Home, get released and run away again. One time I took off when I was outside after taking out the trash, once I ran away from school but the last time I left and was gone for good was the fall of my 10th grade year. I climbed out of the window and jumped off the roof. I packed a laundry basket full of clothes, threw it out the window and as soon as my sister stepped out of the room I climbed out of our bedroom window and just jumped off the roof. I liked to claim that I was escaping an abusive home, but looking back my parents were just trying to do anything they could to save their daughter from a child molester.

Once I ran away he didn't have anywhere to hide me so we just lived at his house that he shared with his mother in a rundown part of the city. That was short lived and eventually she grew weary of her grown son harboring this 15 year old runaway so she moved out on her own and I was left alone in the house for the most part when he would go to work. I would just kind of hide out in there since he was always working one dead end job or another at a local restaurant. What stands out in my mind the most during that time of my life is the hunger. I was always so very hungry. Thinking back, our meal budget seemed to be about $10 a week or so. Edward would go stock pile little Debbie snacks, boxes and boxes of Oatmeal cream pies and Swiss rolls. He would work random odd jobs at pizza shops and we'd get a meal here or there from a messed up order. I remember sitting there day dreaming about toast slathered in butter. I was starving and I just wanted food, some sustenance. But I wasn't hungry enough to go back home and by that point he had me convinced that I was an abused and neglected child so if I went home it would be nothing but torture left for me.

After his mom moved out it wasn't long before we were evicted. We packed up what we could carry and resorted to sleeping in churches, abandon houses, cars, parks, even the Boy Scout church wasn't off limits. He was the leader of a Boy Scout pack at that time and had access to the troop's church. We would slip in late at night and raid the kitchen for anything to eat then sleep for a few hours only to wake up before dawn to sneak back out. There wasn't much to eat inside that building but they did seem to have an inordinate amount of pickles in the refrigerator. After a few nights of that the Church administration quickly found out and made him turn over the keys. No more pickles for me. From there we'd sleep anywhere we could. Walking the streets day in and day out hoping someone would take pity on us and let us stay for a day or 2. Sometimes we would sleep in his pastors van, sometimes we would walk several miles out to the Boy Scout camp where he had a friend named Chip who would let us stay a night or two. Chip always had an open door and an open fridge, and in a time where food was a luxury, I'll always remember his kindness. I happened to run into Chip recently and thanked him for his kindness, he truly had no idea those small gestures of his kindness meant the world to me.

One night we actually slept outside. It was on a picnic table at a Metro park. I used one of those thin silver blankets you can buy from Walmart at the register for like $1.97. We got to the park and I used my arms as a pillow as I sat on the picnic table and covered myself with the blanket. It was so cold, and I swallowed so much air that night that I had a stomach ache when I woke up and honestly those times were completely and utterly miserable. Since Edward was still in the National Guard at the time, he would go on deployments and always come back with a couple MRE's (Meals Ready to Eat). These self-contained food rations of dried meals that soldiers would take into the battlefield to sustain themselves. They were disgusting, but after a day or 2 of not eating any food at all, the spaghetti packets used to taste like a gourmet meal. After a couple months of living basically outdoors, Edward happened to run into an old friend of his who owned property. He let us stay in one of his houses for free. An old dilapidated abandoned (bando) house at the end of a dead end street in one of the worst parts of the city. The house didn't have running water or gas, just electricity. We used a portable toilet that we kept in another room and stayed contained in our bedroom where we had a little heater, an old thin dirty camper mattress and a small black and white TV. This was home, an abandoned house with no utilities, and I was still hungry. But I refused to go back home and by this time I was engaged to him. He had proposed the previous Valentine's Day in 1993 in the most ghetto way possible by taking me to dinner at Ponderosa Steak house and presenting me with a little gold ring with a heart shaped and tiny diamond in the center. I said yes because at the time I believed I actually loved him and could deal with his flaws but the older I got the less I was able to tolerate him. He was bland, weird, oddly obsessed with me and I was always cold hungry or tired or dirty.

I had some friends that I knew from high school who also knew Edward so they let me come live with them while I left him to his own devices in the bando. After a couple years together He had begun drinking cheap gas station alcohol in order to show me how 'cool' he was. He had never drank in the past, and now he was attempting to loosen up but I was pretty much fed up with him at this point. I had just turned 16 and was beginning to catch the eyes of some guys my age. I would repeatedly cheat on him with boys from the neighborhood or school and eventually ended up with a sexually transmitted disease. Or maybe it wasn't a disease more of an annoyance because what I caught was crabs but it was still embarrassing because I had to call him and tell him about it because I had no money to purchase the prescription. But no matter what he always stayed with me because he 'loved' me. I had been a run away for a little over a year now and was realizing just how creepy he actually was and didn't care for him much but I knew the only other alternative was to go back home and there was no way I was doing that. I was staying with my friend's full time for the most part and was warm, fed and having a blast. I couldn't imagine going back to live with my adoptive family at this point even though I deeply missed my siblings. I would risk my freedom by occasionally attempting to sneak to their schools just to talk to them, and even named my pet hamster after my little brother.

But I was also connecting with my black side and learning about the culture and history, the food, and how to fix my hair. I fell in love with my culture and race and I didn't want to lose it by going back into the Cummings home. So going back now was out of the question. I was ready to embrace my ethnicity, to learn how to be a black girl in this world and I just couldn't do it in a home where there wasn't a seasoning to be found. And after spending 12 years eating Shake N Bake burnt bottom chicken legs there was no way I was doing back. I began watching my friends cook and trying to learn everything I could about being black. After several months of watching my friends cook different soul food recipes I felt like I was ready. It all seemed easy enough so I planned my first home cooked meal for Edward. First thing I did was pull some chicken legs out of the freezer and ran them under water just long enough for them to separate then coated them in cornmeal (I later learned this was my first mistake). Then I poured some grease into the pan and made sure to turn the fire up on high so it could cook as quickly as possible since I didn't want my man to wait a second longer for what he was getting ready to experience. Once the grease started smoking I figured it was just about ready for the chicken. I dropped a leg in and the grease erupted. That's the 'perfect temperature' I thought to myself. So I proceeded to drop the remaining 5 pieces of chicken into the grease. That chicken spent the next seven and half minutes getting burnt to a crisp on the outside. Once smoke began coming up from the grease I knew it was finished cooking and I pulled the legs out of the grease one by one and proudly fixed my man his plate and took it to him. I stood there smiling from ear to ear waiting to absorb his praise. He took one bite and looked directly at me then at the chicken that was still bloody raw and half frozen in his hand then back at me and with his eyebrows raised and a look of sheer terror on his face asked me what I had just done. My smile faded to a frown as I realized that every single piece was burnt on the outside and raw in the middle. Thankfully he didn't get sick, but I was banned from cooking in the house ever again. I also realized that I had to lot more to learn to get this whole soul food thing down. I'd also like to add that to this day the smoke detector still regularly goes off when I'm cooking and I still have yet to master the art of cooking soul food. So I've basically just sworn cooking off as much as possible anymore. It's just feels easier this way.

I spent my days hanging with my friends. They had basically taken me in as their own at this point and would let me crash on their couch for months at a time while Edward stayed back at the bando. We would drink and smoke occasionally, play cards watch T.V just normal kid things. A couple of us girls got together and made up our own little clique. The Pretty Girls Click (PGC) is what we called ourselves. There were 4 of us and we would make up dances and have house parties and dance offs while Snoop Dogg's Doggy style played in the background. I remember the guys standing outside of 2 live music, a local record store on the Westside at midnight for that C.D. to come out. Those were the good times man. A little set with a couple friends, all good vibes and nobody pulled a gun out. I guess that's what they mean by the good ol' days huh?

I was faithful for quite a while in the beginning of mine and Edwards's relationship. And in my 14-15 year old mind truly believed I loved him as much as a young girl could love a grown man But as I grew older and spent some time away from him I started seeing boys my age even though I was still technically still engaged to Edward, I began dating and becoming intimate with a few of them. Eventually my carelessness led to me getting pregnant by a neighbor kid that I met through a mutual friend, and I became pregnant after the first and only night we were together. In my young mind the consequences of unprotected sex somehow eluded me and it never even dawned on me that it could actually happen to me. The very next day after we were intimate I began feeling a weird flutter in my stomach and wondered aloud to my friends if that was supposed to happen and if I could be pregnant but we all just laughed together at my foolishness and moved on with our days. But I just felt odd, like there was something happening inside my body and I knew it felt different than anything else I had ever felt and sure enough, several weeks later, when I missed my period, I took a test it came out positive. I was shook. Here I was, sixteen, homeless, uneducated, pregnant, and engaged to a 25 year old man and still a runaway.

I knew immediately that the child I was carrying wasn't Edwards. At that point I hadn't been back to the bando in several weeks let alone slept with him.

He would try to come visit me at my friends by walking literally across town in the middle of winter and I would just send him right back home. I didn't want anything to do with him at this point but I also had no financial means to take care of myself or this child, so when the child's biological father denied the baby when I announced my pregnancy to him, I knew I had no choice but to rely on Edward. Even though he knew from the beginning the child was not biologically his, he 'loved' me so much he was willing to step up, accept the child and raise it as his own. Frankly he was just happy I'd be moving back into the bando with him and becoming solely reliant on him to take care of me and this baby, and he was more than willing to do so. The first few months of my pregnancy I was back and forth between my friend's house and the bando until Edward saved enough money to rent us a house.

It was a little 2 bedroom place a few blocks away from a local hospital and we barely had just enough money to pay the rent. Food and utilities became a luxury again. The gas was off in this home as well leaving us with no heat so I would spend my days heating up water on the stove and taking hot baths to stay warm. My belly was getting bigger and bigger by the day. Despite my circumstances, I was so excited for this baby and I finally had my very own person to love and to love me back. I loved this little baby growing inside me with an intensity and depth that I didn't know was possible and I vowed to him that I would always keep him safe and next to me so he would never ever wonder why his mommy never came back for him. Regardless of my age I would always make sure to figure out a way to take care of him and keep him safe.

I would occupy my time by attending classes at the local pregnancy center to obtain items for my new baby and would sneak into the student resident quarters at the local hospital raiding their kitchens and eating their sack lunches, because although our situation had slightly improved, we still didn't have much in our budget for food yet again. I believe we spent about $25 dollars per week and our diet consisted of boxed pre-pattied hamburgers and a bag of potatoes. I would eat burgers and fries day in and day out to go along with my boiled hot water baths. Despite our tight budget, we still managed to find enough extra money to go out once a week. Every Sunday we would walk the 3 or 4 miles up to the Old Country Buffet at Chapel Hill mall. It was Edwards's favorite place and it was cheap. I would just eat and eat until my stomach hurt and there was no more room for food or baby. I was 6 months pregnant by this point I was absolutely miserable after walking that distance and by the time we made it to the restaurant I would just gorge my famished face until I thought I would burst. After dinner he always wanted to go see a movie and let me tell you, sitting in those seats with a big protruding belly after eating my weight in food was an hour and a half of sheer torture. I would feel absolutely miserable just sitting there watching whatever movie was playing only to get sleepy halfway through then still have to walk the several miles to get back home. There was this advertisement that would play on the screen before any of the movies at that time It featured animated popcorn, a soda cup and a box of Milk Duds playing musical instruments in a band and every single time it came across the big screen on Edward would get the dumbest smile and start be-bopping his head back and forth and moving his arms to the music, then he would laugh amusingly at himself when he was done because he thought it was hysterical to dance along to this commercial every single week. I would just look at him in disgust and repulsion and was beginning to despise him and everything about him. From his laugh to his mannerisms and from his looks to his deep gravelly voice, everything about him was beginning to disgust me.

And to this day, over 30 years later, I still hate going to the movie theater.

Right around that time, about six months into my pregnancy, my parents found out about it through the grapevine and sent a message to me though my extended family. They issued an ultimatum to us that either we marry within 48 hours or they were pressing charges on Edward for statutory rape since I was still underage and visibly pregnant. They said that now they could prove that we were sexually active and I didn't have the heart to tell them the baby wasn't his. I had no plans on telling them either because I figured that would give them leverage to force me to move back home and there was no way I was raising my child within that family. I had my own family now.

So I called their bluff.

Chicken, Cake and I do.

Although I was technically still a runaway, I tried to remain in contact with my extended adoptive family as much as possible. March 14 1994 I had stopped by to visit my twin cousins when I found out about the ultimatum my parents had issued. I made the decision right then and there that I was just going to marry him. I mean it was only marriage and not that big of a deal right? So his mother and I got busy planning the wedding that was set to take place two days later at his Grandfathers home. The elderly man was a local well known preacher and would officiate the ceremony. His mother took me to the local beauty college to get my hair done, and we found one of her old blue church dresses for me to wear. I was almost 7 months pregnant and finding a wedding dress and getting alterations in 48 hours was going to be impossible to find let alone pay for, plus we were still extremely poor and I was still hungry.

We got married within the 48 hour window on March 16, 1994. It was 12 days before my 17th birthday. The ceremony was held in his grandfather's living room in his small ranch style house in West Akron with 3 of my friends in attendance. I wore the blue dress and he wore a Duke Blue devils t-shirt and some Karl Kani shorts. His mother had went out earlier in the day and purchased a cake from a local grocery store, some red juice and a bucket of KFC chicken for our reception dinner that was held in the kitchen that was adjoining the living room. I walked down the aisle (past the couches) and met my groom at the alter (the reclining chair). As the preacher began the ceremony and reading bible verses I busted out laughing. This was absolutely absurd that this was happening right now. I was getting married and all I could do was laugh that it was actually happening. I laughed off and on throughout the entire ceremony up until the preacher looked at me and asked me "Do you take this man to be your lawfully wedded husband till death to you part?". This wasn't funny anymore. I stared at this man and realized that I actually despised him and that I didn't want to spend 15 more minutes with him let alone the rest of my life. In that very moment I understood the sanctity of marriage and how serious it was. And since that very moment, I made a vow that to myself that I would never feel that way standing at an altar ever again. He stood there looking at me with this big dumb grin from ear to ear pleased that he had won his prize. His child bride. In a split second I wondered what would happen if I said "No"., but as I looked over at my friends smiling faces on the couch, my 16 year old mind thought to myself, "if I say NO they're not gonna get any chicken and cake and then they'll be mad at me." I looked back at Edward, took a deep breath and said "I do".

It was done and we were married.

We walked into the kitchen where our reception was being held to celebrate. My friends all seemed so happy for me so I figured I should act happy too, maybe it just needed to settle in for a while or something I thought. As I pretended to bask in the wedded bliss I grabbed the bucket of chicken to pass around. As I offered the food, my friends all looked at me with their hands placed over their stomachs and said "Oh no! No thank you, we've been eating chicken all week. Baked chicken, boiled chicken, fried chicken, chicken fricassee." My heart dropped. I thought to myself "you mean to tell me I just said "I do" so ya'll can have some chicken and cake and ya'll aren't even going to eat the chicken and cake?"

I felt sick and immediately trapped.

I guess you could say we settled into married life. We moved into an apartment by his mom and he had secured a better job that allowed for rent and food to be had simultaneously. I tried to learn to like him again, I really did. But by this point I was only with him because I was in my last trimester and didn't have many options. I had a few friends who were also pregnant at the same time I was and while I was watching their families throw them baby showers bombarded with brand new gifts for their babies while I was taking classes at the local pregnancy center to earn enough vouchers to get a used car seat but I was having a baby and he was going to be loved so none of that mattered. I had a little support from my friends I had stayed in contact with from high school and a few family members but not a big support system by any means but none of that mattered either as I was so excited for this baby. My pregnancy was fairly smooth with no sickness or complications, not even a drop of heartburn but I gained quite a bit of weight, almost 85 lbs. to be exact and I'm not sure how since we always seemed to be hungry. My doctors gave me a due date of June 26, 1994 and being 17 and knowing nothing about how labor or birthing worked,

I just assumed that on June 26th I was going to have a baby. So on my due date I arrived at the hospital with my packed bags and walked into labor and delivery. I informed them that today was my due date and I was there to have my baby. They looked at me bewildered and asked if I was experiencing any contractions or water rupture. I responded "no" but since the doctor told me that today was my due date, I was ready to have my baby. They chucked and explained to me what the laboring process looks and feels like and told me to go home until I began to show signs of active labor.

The contractions began later that night as I laid in bed contemplating how long this baby could live inside me while stimulating my nipples trying to induce labor. After about 5 min of playing with my breasts I felt a cramp in my uterus. It didn't really hurt but I felt it so I kept going. The pains continued to come and began to intensify. I waited a bit before I told Edward I was in labor and we began to time the contractions. It didn't take long to reach 5 min apart so 12 hours later we headed back to the hospital. Labor was painful but for the most part went smoothly, but as it neared time for me to push the doctors noticed some distress in the fetal heart monitor. The doctor attempted to insert some type of wired device into my uterus to attach to the baby's head to keep close tabs on baby but after 2 attempts the doctor looked at me and said "this kid has more hair then me, I can't get it to stick anywhere on his head". I wasn't sure what he meant and I also didn't care as I had already been in labor for hours and just wanted it to be over. Finally, once the baby's heart rate went back to normal and after several pushes I gave birth to a 7lb 13 oz. baby boy who was absolutely perfect.

He had big brown eyes and literally had the most hair I'd ever seen on a baby even to this day. He had about 2 inches of thick curly hair covering his entire head, not a bald or missing patch anywhere, I mean this kid had a ridiculous amount of hair but he was absolutely adorable and I was completely in love with him. He was a calm quiet baby and really didn't fuss much at all. He also looked just like the other guy, I mean absolutely identical. Edward attempted to save face and bring a baby picture of himself to the hospital to prove to himself and our friend's that this was in fact his baby. They placated him and told him exactly what his little heart wanted to hear, that the baby looked just like him in an attempt to justify his foolishness but after he left the room we laughed and laughed at how stupid he was to actually believe that.

I was discharged from the hospital and was settling into life as a new mother. I didn't know much about babies except from what I had seen while helping my adopted mom babysit and was still learning as I went. We had been home for about 2 weeks when my newborn began vomiting a dark green substance. Even though I didn't know much about babies I instinctually knew this wasn't right. He wasn't showing any signs of distress like crying or a fever since he actually didn't cry at all his first few weeks. When he was hungry he would lay there like a baby bird opening his mouth over and over. I would set an alarm for every 3 hours to feed him because he just didn't cry so when he began to vomit I rushed him to the hospital. On three separate occasions over the course of as many days they sent me home stating that it was typical baby vomit and to give him Pedialite. He wasn't vomiting profusely and since he wasn't lethargic they said he would be fine. On the final visit to the emergency room I demanded we be seen and they placed us in a room with a camera installed to monitor me as if I was harming him in some way to cause his vomiting. Of course they found nothing and just as the last doctor was about to discharge us my son vomited again. The doctor looked at me stunned as I explained that this is what has been happening. After a quick examination and X-ray the doctor found that my baby had a double hernia that was blocking his bowel and he would need to have surgery immediately. Edward was overseas on a National Guard deployment and I was alone with the baby in the hospital. He was so tiny and I was so scared for him. He was admitted for surgery and remained for 3 days and I stayed by his side the entire time not even leaving to change or shower. I didn't have much family I could call on for support so I spent most of the time alone.

I did attempt to reconnect with my adopted mom at this time but it was short lived once she began telling me how to care for the baby and being overbearing as usual. By the time he was released Edward still wasn't home from his deployment so. I decided to have a friend take me and the baby over to his biological father's house to meet him. He looked at him and instantly knew that was his son and begged me leave Edward and let him be a father, but I was married now and because of that Edward was on his birth certificate and legally his father and there wasn't anything I could do about that so I just moved on with my life and didn't see him again after that. Now that my son was on the mend and Edward was back from Deployment, I got a job at a telemarking company selling the Ron Popiel automatic pasta maker and reenrolled myself back in high school. I was able to enroll into the 11th grade and made every attempt to still graduate on time. I would wake up, dress myself and the baby, get on the bus to drop him off at the sitters that was right around the corner from my high school, pick him up afterwards and go home and spend the evenings dong homework and playing with my baby. I would also still hang out with my group of friends occasionally and get drunk or go to concerts.

October of 1995, Bone Thugs and Harmony was performing in Akron at a small local theater and my friends and I got tickets. There was about 5 or 6 of us that went and somehow we ended up back at the hotel with them after the concert. They had several room and the group's members were coming in and out of each room. As the night wore on I became restless sitting in this hotel room with my friends while they flirted with the roadies and a couple of the Bones. I had just given birth to my son and was overweight, frumpy with crunchy hair and just all around impoverished looking, they weren't giving me a 2nd glance but I totally had the hots for Flesh n Bone. I called my husband to come pick me up and gave him the room number. Since this was a time before cellphones he had to way to contact me once he arrived. He pulled up and was walking to the room knocking and searching for me and ran into Flesh and asked him my whereabouts. The rapper responded he didn't know where or who I was and just kept walking. After an hour passed I called again to see why he hadn't retrieved me and he said he had just left after being told I wasn't there. I gave him the room number again and told him to knock on the door when he arrived. When he finally knocked on the door, it just happened to be Flesh that opened the door and my husband instantly flipped out on him cursing and yelling that he lied to him. They got into a verbal altercation as we all just sat there staring with our mouths open, we couldn't believe he had just gotten into an argument with Flesh n Bone. I got up to leave before the situation escalated and myself and 3 of my friends left with him that night while leaving 2 of our other friends behind. To this day they have never confessed to sleeping with any of the Bones but the rest of us have had our serious suspicions, especially when they became excited about the prospect of the band sending those memorabilia the following day when they eventually made it back home.

My constant cheating eventually led me into the arms and bed of one of my classmates and we began seeing each other. I would leave my 5 month old baby in day care just a little bit longer and go hang out at his house. Eventually I would just stay there until the evening leaving Edward to pick up the baby from daycare. He was either oblivious, blind or both to not see that I was dealing with another guy yet again. I would have him pick me up from this guy's house in the evenings saying I was doing homework. I was no longer intimate with Edward for several reasons so I began having unprotected sex with the other guy on a daily basis. I would spend time with him through the week then go out and date other guys on the weekends. One night I was with a girlfriend and she needed a plus 1. It was me and her and 2 guys and we were just drinking a little bit and hanging out. As the alcohol kicked in one of the men began making sexual advances towards me. I told him as long as he wore protection I would have sex with him so off to his grandma's basement we went. At first our intercourse seemed like normal regular condom sex, nothing special but I specifically remember him pulling out for several seconds then reentering me before climaxing. I had no idea what he had just done and was too naïve and scared to ask, so when we finished I went on my merry way. About 10 days later I felt a familiar flutter and took another pregnancy test only to discover I was pregnant yet again. This time was not by my husband either but I assumed it was my classmate's baby because that was the only person I had unprotected sex with. I informed him of the pregnancy and while he was hesitant to believe the baby was his due to my reputation, he still attempted to maintain contact with me until the baby arrived just in case it was.

I was nowhere near ready for another baby. Not emotionally mentally physically or financially. I considered abortion or adoption but I knew I never ever wanted to end up like my biological mother and abandon my child so I did what I needed to do to prepare for this baby. But I wasn't exactly sure what to do now with two kids at 18 years old. No diploma, no job, and no way to make the amount of money it would take to raise two babies especially without fathers. I was extremely reluctant to tell Edward and I hid my pregnancy symptoms and waited several weeks to do so until early November. We had been working on 'improving' and 'repairing' our relationship and one night, as we lay on the living room floor listening to the Above the Rim soundtrack and disusing how we were going to work on rebuilding our relationship I revealed that I was pregnant again for a 2nd time and this child was not his either. He laid there quietly for a moment, sat up, looked at me, put his shoes on and walked right out the front door and never came back.

Days after he left I eventually got wind that he was living with a mutual female friend in West Akron and I actually had the nerve to act distraught and suicidal. I knew damn well I didn't want to be with this man, but yet one night I called emergency services in distress and sadness and told the paramedics that I wanted to jump in front of a bus so I was committed to the psychiatric unit at a local hospital on a 72 hour hold. I sent my infant son to stay with his my husband and his new girlfriend while I figured out my next steps. And by the time I was released I was ready to move on with my life. So I picked up my baby, packed up our belongings moved in with a family friend. . I was able to live with her and her family for the better part of a year while I was on the waiting list for low income housing. I worked and prepared for this new baby and tried to keep a positive mindset despite my circumstances. My son was growing and was the cutest most cherub baby you could ask for. With a head full of soft curly hair, eyelashes that were dark and long, chubby cheeks and a bright smile he was absolutely adorable and I loved being his mother. He was extremely smart and advanced for his age walking at 8.5 months. He was an easy going and laid back baby who hated having to get his hair combed and it was becoming unmanageable because there was just so much of it. As easy as it was to parent him because he was an all-around easy baby and I loved being a mom, the thought of being alone with 2 babies was terrifying. I wasn't ready for another baby. Not at all. But I knew in the end that these were my babies and matter what and I would do whatever it took to take care of them both.

Being pregnant while having a young child is not for the faint at heart. This pregnancy was rough on me and took its toll on my body. It caused me to gain quite a bit of weight and by the time I gave birth in the middle of summer of 1995 I was 100 lbs. over my pre pregnancy weight. That was a hot miserable summer and you couldn't seem to escape the heat especially at 9 months pregnant. I gave birth to a 9lb 4 oz. baby girl in July of that year that I named Imani. She came out with a fighting spirit that she still carries to this day. Although I was ecstatic I had a healthy baby, I also wasn't expecting such a large baby. When I tried to dress her to take her home from the nursery we couldn't even button her clothing so she had to wear a hospital gown. She was very fussy as a newborn, very colicky and was changed to several formulas before we found the right one that soothed her achy tummy. She wasn't snuggly or cuddly like my son and didn't care much to be held or rocked. She preferred to sleep in her swing at night but the swings in those day weren't battery operated or electric, they were crank swings and every 20-30 min you'd have to get up and re-crank the loud lever for the swing to keep swinging. It was daunting and exhausting caring for both of the babies. Especially when you have a fussy newborn who is crying every half hour to either eat or be swung, it doesn't take long for sheer fatigue to kick in so needless to say the early months of mothering a 13 month old and a newborn were absolutely unpleasant, so my son would spend part of his week my ex-husband as it just made life easier not having 2 babies to care for all the time. I had my daughter full time but I didn't mind. She was such a sweet meek baby who was very inquisitive and sensitive. As she got older she didn't seem to care much for her older brother and as soon as she was mobile she would spend every second she could antagonizing him, pulling his hair or hitting him with toys. She was bigger than him and she would bully him and when you would scold her she would give you the most rotten smile with her nose and lips tooted up. Once she grew out of her colicky phase she became a hit among all my friends. She was absolutely adorable and they loved to show her off. They eventually began proclaiming her as their daughter as well and would keep her for several days at a time taking care of her as their own.

The one particular friend that would tote her around endlessly happened to run into one of her former boyfriends while she was out with my daughter one day. He also happened to be the man that introduced me to her suspected father that fateful evening as well. Although my friend had been messing around with him off and on for several months before we all linked up the night my daughter was possibly conceived and she hadn't seen him in well over a year. When she ran into him with my daughter in tow he inquired as to whose baby it was, she told him that my daughter was in fact their baby. He was devastated that she had kept the pregnancy hidden from him and his family until after she was born and made it his mission to provide every way he could by purchasing clothes, diapers, a playpen and a stroller. His mother and grandmother were also under the assumption that this was their child and would ask over and over if they could babysit or if she could come over for a few hours. After several weeks it was becoming overwhelming and difficult to keep the lies going. Even after my friends s own grandmother told them to their face that she had never given birth and that wasn't even her child the family didn't care. They were relentless in their pursuit of loving my child and it wasn't until my friend furnished her birth documentation that I had given her to show them did they finally realize that the baby wasn't theirs.

As I waited to receive my housing I worked with Child Support to establish paternity of my daughter. They reached out to my former classmate and he took a DNA test. Several weeks later the results came back that we was not my daughter's father. That left me with one other person and I specifically remember using protection with him that night. After talking with some friends we concluded that he was removing the condom when he was repositioning himself or whatever he said he was doing. I tracked him down to the house I had met him at and he revealed that he had just had twin's several days prior to my daughter's birth, and since he was in a relationship with the infant's mother, he wasn't interested in taking a DNA test for my child. I left him standing right there on his doorstep and we never seen him again.

To this day he has never met my daughter.

Diapers and Weed

I didn't have many options for housing being an underemployed eighteen year old with two babies. I picked up a job at a local pizza shop and despite repeatedly cheating on her son, my mother in law was able to secure me temporary housing with a friend of hers. The woman was also a single mother of four children and she allowed me to rent out a room in her home free of charge. My son would spend most of the week with Edward and the weekends with me. The arrangement worked out well considering my circumstances and I lived with the family for approximately nine months while I waited for my name to come up subsidized housing waiting list.

Growing up fairly sheltered, I had never experienced "life in the hood" and had no idea what the next year would have in store for me. My name was finally up on the housing wait list and I was informed that there was an apartment ready for me and my children. The rent was $1 per month and we moved in November 3 of 1995. Myself, my 2 children aged 2 yrs. and 4 months at the time and my best friend Niechelle. Although we knew each other from high school we recently struck up a friendship. Chelle is an absolutely gorgeous woman. She's got a deep caramel complexion with exotic facial features. Slightly slanted eyes with jet black hair and perfectly straight white teeth. She has a unique and striking face and the shapeliest ass I've ever seen on a woman even to this day. She adored my children as their aunt and they loved her for it. Our apartment was a 2 story 3 bedroom 1 ½ bath in the Rosemary projects on the East side of Akron. The housing complex holds about 350-400 units over several acres of land. It sits across from a plaza and is tucked behind several fast food restaurants and a small tree lining. The apartments are identical to each other with brick on the bottom and white siding on the top. The inside touted dark brown carpet and white walls with 1 ½ baths. A standard apartment by all accounts. The 3 bedrooms were upstairs all on the right side of the hall way with the bathroom at the end of the hall. Since we moved in during the winter, the evenings were generally quiet. Niechelle and I spent our time playing with my growing babies and working towards obtaining our GED's Neither of us managed to graduate high school so we worked hard on studying for the test and bot passed in January of 1996. It wasn't long after we'd completed our education that we met the group of people who would forever change our lives. And not for the better.

We had begun hanging out at local clubs and although I don't recall exactly how we all connected with each other that fateful night, but we became almost inseparable for the next 8 months. Their names were Tony and Tyrone. Toney was the luscious locked singer of a music group with a Tevin Campbell vibe, and he was performing with a local aspiring rapper Tyrone. We struck up a friendship immediately with them and rather quickly we began traveling to their concerts with them and were mesmerized by what we were being exposed to. The clubs, people, the VIP treatment. People seemed to know Tyrone everywhere we went and they loved him. We were hanging out with R&B groups like the Rude Boyz and Levert and I'm pretty positive I dated Bingo for a short bit. Of course with our new found fame Niechelle and I had to look the part. We changed the way we dressed and did out hair and somehow stumbled across these gaudy puffy winter coats in a nearby store. Hers was patent leather white, and mine was silver, and both were oddly shiny in their own ways and truly just God awful coats. But we were young, beautiful and had life by the balls in our shiny puffy coats.

Drinking and getting high became almost a daily occurrence which led to my time with my children becoming less and less. I began to ship them off to anyone who would be willing to babysit while I club hopped and attempted to fit in how ever I could. Although I was unemployed I managed to find ways to have enough money to party as often as my little heart desired. Every night of the week there was a different club to go to, Bubs place, B&J's, Rob Roy's, and Hogg Heaven. When we weren't out in clubs we would be finding ways to entertain ourselves inside. One of our favorite games to play was hide and seek in the dark while drunk. We had played this several times before without any issues and would always end up laughing our asses off at the places people managed to hide inside the tiny apartment. Playing around as usual one night we were all running through the darkened apartment when we hear a loud scream and thud at the bottom of the steps. We raced to the sound and turned on the lights only to find that our 3rd roommate Shani who had moved in recently had missed the last 2 steps and hit her face on the door. It knocked her front tooth out. She was rushed to emergency only to come back with a humongous knot on her lip that prevented her from opening her mouth all of the way. She would eat Taco bell by ripping the tacos into pieces, tilting her head back and dropping the pieces into her mouth. We lovingly and hysterically referred to her as Monkey Mouth for several weeks after the accident. We also didn't play that game anymore after that.

Summer had arrived and we were young, fine, and build like shit brick houses, each of us extremely curvy in our own ways. We knew everybody it seemed, and our social life was flourishing. We had the "cool house" in the projects where EVERYBODY linked up at. My children were an afterthought at this point. I was barely visiting them let alone parenting them in any capacity and even when they were home I didn't have any food to feed them anyways. Id sell my food stamps to have money to drink and party. Plus we always seemed to have a steady stream of new 'roommates'. Random people that would just end up living with us somehow for a few weeks to a few months, I was in no condition or position to be a good mother and the day THAT particular realization hit me was just a random weekday. My daughter had just turned one and the heat of the summer had kicked in. I had spent my afternoon smoking blunts with friends while my children napped. They both woke up hungry as any child would, searching for lunch. I combed my refrigerator for ANYTHING to put together to feed these 2 hungry babies. All I had was left over tuna casserole from 2 nights before and little else because I regularly sold my food stamp allotment to purchase alcohol and marijuana and any other money that I got from donating plasma (Forty dollars per week) went to purchasing weed and diapers. . I tried my hardest to doctor it make it edible because there was simply nothing else for me to put together. I threw it in a pan and added some water and seasonings and as I handed my babies these bowls of old reheated food, my 2 yr. old son looks at me with his big eyes and long lashes and begins to cry. "I want food mommy". There was nothing, I had no food to feed them and I felt intense shame, disgust and horror as I sat there high as a kite looking at my helpless babies. They both had dirt on their sweet little faces and were wearing the same clothes from the previous day and just looked all around sad and traumatized from the life I was providing them. Then I looked around at my surroundings and was completely sickened at what I was seeing.

The apartment was absolutely disgusting with dark dirt stains embedded into the carpet, a wooden dining room table doubled as an entertainment stand that held a small old color T.V with rabbit ears. For furniture we had an old hand me down Victorian looking couch and a couple milk crates and small toy box in the corner held the few toys the kids had left at this point. The apartment was filthy and was dubbed "under the bridge" by our friends because It was akin to living in squalor. Absolutely disgusting. Trash overflowing, dirty walls and definitely no place for a child to thrive. It was 2 pm on a Tuesday and I was extremely high with 2 crying hungry dirty toddlers with nothing to feed them. What kind of life is this I thought to myself? I began sobbing and asking them to forgive me. My heart broke for my beautiful babies. They deserved better. They deserved food and a HOME and a responsible mother who didn't foolishly sell her food stamps to purchase drugs cigarettes and alcohol. But I had no idea how to give them that because I was still searching for my own home in this world and couldn't even give myself the love and care that I myself needed at that time. I'm sure I was able to feed them somehow that day, but from that moment forward, the effects and smell of marijuana gave me the most intense bouts of paranoia that stayed with me for decades after that day.

The summer of '96 progressed. Tupac had been released from prison and All Eyez on Me was released and it became an instant cult classic. I was beginning to get a reputation in the projects and couldn't figure out how I just kept on having sex with these guys. It took me years to realize that when they would ask me "what's up with me tonight" that was there code for "can I fuck'? God I was unbelievably naïve to that life. And the men? Lemme tell ya'll about these men. There was the one guy who took off his shoes and the odor stunk up the entire upstairs and my friends told me afterwards they thought the smell was my vagina, this same guy also told me he was hired hit man for the Yakuza Japanese Mob. I believed him. Then there was the one guy who came so quickly during sex that when I came downstairs my friends thought I was coming to ask for a condom. Then there was the guy in the wheelchair. He was an older guy and I had met him through a mutual friend. He couldn't obtain an erection and he immensely enjoyed oral sex. It was the middle of summer and I was at his apartment. I didn't drive at the time so he had picked me up. As the day went on and he continuously performed oral sex on me I became irritated and sore and asked him to take me home but he refused and continued attempting to perform oral sex on me for hours and trying to force my legs apart. I was enraged and left the room heading to the kitchen to find something to eat while I waited for him to take me home. In the refrigerator I stumbled across some fresh fish he had caught the previous day so I took one out and began to cut it into small pieces. I then proceeded to place the pieces in spots all over his apartment that I knew he couldn't reach. Behind the stove, behind the refrigerator, up on the top of the windows and under his car seats. In the middle of the heat of summer it was just a matter of time before the inevitable stench overtook his senses. He never called me again after that day.

There were always so many people in and around us at this time and it felt like we knew everybody so on this particular day when a one of the homies pulled up it wasn't much more different than any of the other days. The kids were shuffled away and I had gotten dressed for the day and ready for whatever. I donned my tan spandex dress and dark brown strappy sandals and around 6 in the evening and I heard a car pull up. Our typical behavior when this happened would be to step outside and see who it is so I did that and I recognized he driver. He was a dude that I was familiar with from the hood. A lower level gang member. I didn't know him well but he seemed nice so when he asked me if I wanted to ride along so I just hopped in the car and took off. We ended up at a hotel not far from my apartment. We went inside and just kind of chilled out for a bit. He started making sexual advances and me, being a naïve people pleaser I ended up having sexual intercourse with him. The room had a double bed and we were in the bed furthest from the wall. As I was getting up to get dressed, one of his friends popped up. He had been hiding between the bed and the wall. When he stood up he demanded I have sex with him. I refused and attempted to grab my clothing to continue getting dressed but he grabbed my clothing before I could reach it. He told me that unless I had sex with him, he would throw my clothes on the roof of the hotel and I would have to walk out naked. I was mortified and afraid. 19 years old and I'm standing here stark naked in this hotel room with 2 men who I did not actually know.

I had recently been placed on probation and I was fearful that if I ran to the front desk with no clothing and the police showed up that I would be arrested. I grabbed a towel to wrap around me. A small white hotel towel that barely covered the front of my body. I attempted to get out the door, only to have another man walk in carrying a camcorder and recording the entire incident. They laughed as they continued to rip the towel off me while still recording. Over and over. No matter what I grabbed. A pillow, another towel, my hands. They reached over and ripped it away while laughing and taunting me while continuously recording. I was sobbing and begging to leave and I don't remember much after those moments. I truly do not recall if I had sex with the man filming and I also do not know if that tape is still floating around out here.

What I do know that when I made it home that evening the usual people were there, Niechelle, Tyrone, his sister Sharon and her boyfriend Mike. I sobbed as I explained to them what happened earlier in the day, they were all obviously shocked at what I was relaying to them. I tried to relax and not think about it but that night, there was more traffic than usual in my apartment so it made it difficult to truly sit and absorb what had just happened to me. People I had never seen before were coming and going, speaking in hushed tones and being very secretive. I really didn't pay it much attention because I was exhausted and just wanted to go to bed to forget the whole situation ever happened.

The next morning, in my normal routine as I sat outside on the stoop, smoking cigarettes and checking out the hood, one of the men from the previous day in the motel came walking up to me. I was a bit frightened thinking he was going to attempt to encourage me to meet up with him again but as he got closer I could see that he was visibly upset. He began frantically yelling at me "What the fuck happened to Tommy? Who killed him? I just kind of sat there stone faced in shock staring at him wondering what he was talking about. I had just woken up I surely didn't know anything about anyone being dead. After calming him down (the irony that was calming one of my rapists down for him finding out the other one dead is not lost on me). Durrell confirmed that earlier that morning Tommy was found by the janitor of a local elementary school. He had been murdered by gunshot wound to his head and his body was found in the parking lot. As the days went on his friends and family pressed us for information, but we truly didn't know the circumstances of the murder and could only speculate. We had our suspicions but we didn't dare ask. We had Tommy's friends and family grilling us for information and we had several of the people who had been in and out of the apartment that night threatening us that if we revealed any information about what we seen that night that there would be consequences. Eventually one of the people that had been coming and going out of the apartment the previous night was arrested, charged and found guilty of the murder. All of our roommates and long term 'guests' left the apartment shortly after that day and nothing was the same after that.

The end of that summer my time spent being a mother and raising my children became less and less. I had found an almost permanent baby sitter for my daughter and my son was with my ex-husband part time so I did what any logical 19 year old would do and I picked up a sugar daddy. A random 65 year old white man I had met who owned a wealth management company, drove a Mark VIII, and owned a mini mansion in Bath. He was fascinated with Yanni and introduced me to my first vibrator. He would take me to the mall and buy me whatever I wanted which was typically just new clothes and shoes but he had an affinity for ball gowns and always wanted to buy me one. I couldn't figure out for the life of me what I would do with a ball gown in the projects, so I would always decline the offer. He liked to dress me up and show me off so the first time he took me to get my hair done I allowed him to pick the style. He picked a short box cut and the barber just buzzed my hair right off. I had about 1 inch of straight hair all over my head just standing up. No style no fade no nothing, just a 1 inch straight frizzy afro all over my head. My friends tried to lie and tell me that it was cute but I knew that it looked crazy. My hair had been bone straight my entire life but from that haircut on, when my hair did begin to grow back it came in extremely curly. I had never had curly hair ever in my life so this was a whole new experience in trying to find the right products to moisturize it. Plus I was still pulling it out so it was patchy in a lot of areas. I eventually began to wear glue in weaves to hide the damage. After several weeks of dating him I realized I wasn't cut out for having a sugar daddy. It felt so gross and plus I didn't find him remotely attractive so I ended the situation. I never did master the art of gold digging.

Fall was arriving and the air was becoming crisp and cool and the leaves were starting to turn from green to beautiful hues of red, orange and yellow. We had become accustomed to life in the projects, I mean it was quite traumatizing but we had adapted. I don't recall how the idea came about, I just know by the fall of 1996 I was introduced to stripping. Little did I know is that I would end up working in the adult industry off and on for the next decade. The closest bar within walking distance was this place was called Chasers. It was across from the now abandoned Rubber Bowl, our local football stadium that's now old, dilapidated, covered in graffiti and used by dirt bikers and motorcyclists as a safe place to ride. Inside Chasers there were 2 sides to the bar. The side where alcohol was sold and consumed the girls would dance in bikinis or little outfits but the other side that was called a juice bar where the dancers could go fully nude. I packed my dance bag, walked the mile and a half to work and walked inside but I wasn't prepared for what my eyes would see when they adjusted to the darkness in the club. As I was escorted to the dressing room I passed a row of drunken men sitting on the bar stools who made comments about the "fresh meat" coming in. I was extremely shy and timid and wasn't sure how I was going to be able to even do this but I took a deep breath, got dressed and walked out past the row of men and into what would become the next decade of my life. The room was full of lights, poles and half naked women who were so loud, full of life and seemed to love the job. Some were standing around talking to men, some were dancing for men on the couches in different stages of undress. "Oh my god I thought how am I ever going to do this I was scared shitless. How will I ever get to the top of that pole? What if they all say no to me? How do I do this? Do they just come pick me or do I have to talk to them?" I was so confused about the entire process. One of the first dancers I met that night was a girl named Rosa, a short sexy Italian girl with large breasts that she would cover with hot candle wax during her set. I was mesmerized. I sat there watching and wondering how she became so sexy and confident. As I sat in a chair in a corner quietly observing I was approached by another dancer named Monet. She was a tall skinny loud black girl who would either hug you or try to cut you depending on the day. We talked for a bit and they assured me after a few drinks I wouldn't even feel any shame or fear and to just go for it. And so it began. After a few days and several drinks later I was laughing stripping and licking my nipples along with the rest of the girls.

My need for constant validation from men was continuing to put me in some compromising situations not only sexually but physically. I had been working at the bar for several weeks at this point and fall was slowly turning into winter. I was still on probation for the trespassing charge I had received earlier that summer when I was introduced by a family friend to a man named Dee. He lived in Detroit and he and I began speaking regularly on the phone. We didn't have social media or cell phones in 1996, so neither of us had a way to get a picture of the other so I went in to this completely blind. After speaking for about a week we decided I would take the Greyhound to Detroit and he'd pick me up from the bus station. Id identify him by his puffy silver coat and light skin. After missing my first bus due to being hungover, I finally made it to Detroit later that day around 7 pm. He picked me up and we went off to our room at a local extended stay. It was a Thursday and the only reason I remember is because I was on probation and had an appointment with my PO that following Monday so I needed to be back in Akron. The room was standard extended stay hotel and he had some friends there when I arrived. The room was full of marijuana smoke, alcohol and random men bagging up drugs on a coffee table. I had never seen such an abundance of drugs before and I was shocked, but nothing could have prepared me for what I would see coming down the stairs a few moments later. One of his friends was carrying an alligator. A 3 foot long gator that he kept as a pet and not only did he carry it around, he also let it roam freely around the room and the other guests didn't even bat an eye. I don't recall what we did those first 2 days in the room but I'm sure in included a lot of drinking drugs and sex. The following Saturday he informed that me we would be checking out of the hotel and going back to his house. I didn't mind as long as I'd be back to the Greyhound station on time to cache my bus back home the following day. Detroit. The east side off Schoolcraft. I had never been there before and was absolutely shocked that there was a liquor store on every corner and bars on all the windows and doors. In Akron there's 1-2 in any given neighborhood, not every corner. Small town girl in big city I guess. We ended up at his house. A small colonial house that matched every other house in that area. Nothing special. Just a small house in the hood on the eastside of Detroit. With bars on the windows and doors as well. We walked inside. Again I had never seen anything like it. The house was dilapidated with peeling paint and huge holes in the walls. There was no furniture in the living room and in the dining room there was a table and chairs and 1 tall bar stool. I was weirded out but not enough to ask to leave, in his bedroom there was a full size mattress and box spring on the floor a side table and a console table with a television on it. There was a phone that was plugged into the wall next to the bed. I called my friends and let them know that I was at his house with him and that to expect me home the next day. We ordered takeout that night and just hung out and when I woke up the next day expecting to get ready to leave, I realized that I was alone and Dee wasn't in bed with me any longer. I look over and see money lying on the nightstand next to the bed. Thinking he was somewhere else in the house, I stepped out of the bedroom only to find a young black male about 17 yrs. old sitting on the bar stool. Not moving not reading just sitting there on the bar stool. When I asked where Dee went and the kid said he's out handling his business and he'll be back. I tried not to worry too much because I knew he remembered that I needed to be at the bus station in a few hours. Hours passed and I was becoming anxious and upset that he hadn't returned and the kid on the chair didn't seem to have any answers, he just sat in that chair the entire day doing nothing but sitting. When I realized he wasn't making it back in time I began to panic that I would receive a probation violation and be returned to jail. Even if I attempted to catch a cab to the Greyhound station I had no way to even get out of this house, as the steel barred door was locked with a key. Day turned into night I was calling home frantically trying to figure out how to get out of the house. Eventually I resigned to the fact that I wasn't making it back home that night, so I just ordered a pizza not even thinking of the steel bars on the door because once it was delivered the box had to be turned sideways to get through the bars leaving the cheese stuck to the top of the box. Night came and still no Dee and the kid was still sitting there. He finally came back in about 2 am and when I told him I'd missed my bus he apologized and said he'd take me first thing the following day and I went to sleep feeling relieved only to wake up the next day discovering that I was again alone in the bed with some money sitting on the table, but this time with no phone. The phone was now in the other room sitting next to the boy on the bar stool and Dee was gone again. I was panicked. How am I going to get out of this house? I can't call the police because I'm on probation and wasn't even supposed to leave the state AND the kid on the barstool has the phone now. I was angered and frustrated but not quite worried yet. I managed to get the phone to order take out while the kid in the chair carefully watched me and figured I'd confront Dee when he got home. Again he arrives through the door late that night and apologizes and tells me he will take me in the morning that he's been dealing with some personal things. I believed him and fell asleep with my bag packed and waiting by the door.

Wednesday I woke up expecting to leave but the day only brought more of the same. Dee gone, money on the table, the kid in the chair. I was livid and becoming frightened but Dee had come back to the house this day exceptionally early so I assumed he was there to take me to the bus station.

As I walked out of the room I quickly understood why the large holes were in the walls and why the young man sat in the chair for several hours a day. Dee reached into one of the walls and pulled out more crack cocaine that I had ever seen in my life. Several gallon sized zip lock bags full of crack cocaine were filling the walls. If I'm going to be completely honest when I saw that I was completely turned on. Not because I wanted the crack, but because I had hit the mother lode of drug dealers. The real deal, not these little nickel and dime brotha's that I was exposed to and at this point I'm starting to wonder how long I can stay in Detroit until probation finds out.

By Thursday I was able to use the phone long enough to be able to connect with the family friend who had introduced us. He and Dee agreed that if I carried a significant amount of rocked crack cocaine back with me, I would be able to take the next bus back to home. So later that day I boarded the Greyhound back to Akron with a bag sandwich bag half full of crack shoved inside my vagina. Talk about painful, them little rocks hurt and that thin tiny bag offered no cushioning they just kept poking me. I tried to sit with one leg propped up but that hurt too then I started to get paranoid wondering if drug dogs would be brought on. It was intense. But finally, after a 3.5 hour bus ride, I made it back to my apartment exhausted and dumbfounded.

Life went back to normal for about a week after I got back. By this time I had been hired into an all nude club called Lisa's Cabaret and was just trying to go on with my life. Several days after I returned home, I came home from work one night and opened my front door to find that my apartment had been broken into, ransacked and had the words REDRUM written on the walls. The place was demolished. Along with the writing on the wall there was flour thrown everywhere along with the usual disarray and filth of the home. I immediately assumed it was Dee since upon my return home I began receiving harassing calls from him stating I stole a diamond ring from him. I honestly never seen the ring in the house but I decided in that moment that I needed to leave that apartment. I wasn't safe there any longer and I had to get out of there. The next day I called my parents to come pick up my daughter who was 16 months now, I packed a few bags for myself and left everything else behind. I didn't know where I was going, but anywhere had to be better than that apartment. I had been sexually assaulted and humiliated, physically assaulted, taken advantage of, caught up in a murder and held captive in another state. I moved out of the Rosemary projects Nov 3, 1996, 1 year exactly to the day that I moved in and ended up moving into a homeless shelter for women.

I arrived at the shelter later that week with only a couple bags of clothes, no money and no plan. I also had no idea what was going to happen from here on out, but I knew it had to be better than the past year. I began adjusting to shelter life and making friends and trying to figure out what was next for me. I wasn't able to continue my career as an exotic dancer while living in the shelter so I began taking courses at the local University for Marketing/ Advertising and had dreams of being a powerful Marketing executive in New York, despite not knowing a single thing about Marketing or how it worked. I began getting involved in organizations on campus and became the secretary of a program tailored to Black students and their barriers to success. The shelter was Christian run that had had fairly strict rules such as attending two church services a day in order to partake in meal service and curfew was 6:30 pm daily. Occasionally you could obtain an overnight pass but that typically reserved for emergencies. I lived in the shelter for about 6 months before one of my friends name was up on the housing list and got an apartment in this old run down motel turned apartments that was next to the shelter. I gave up my bed in the shelter to stay with her for a while. It was small, cramped and dank in them apartments and was littered with drugs. Outside of alcohol and weed I still didn't know much about drugs and my year in the Rosemary had only slightly prepared me for life in 'the streets'. This was the first time I had witnessed someone doing cocaine in front of me, and watching him snort that powder white line up his nose then looking at his eyes as they turned big as saucers scared the shit out of me. I couldn't figure out how the powder didn't burn his brain and it freaked me out the way his eyes got really bit and I decided then and there that cocaine was not for me. Since it was a small studio apartment I would visit with my children at a park or McDonalds for the next several months until I eventually just moved back into the shelter. As bad as the shelter rules sucked, I was still receiving three meals a day, having my physical needs met and able to visit with my children in a safe place... While I was temporarily back in the shelter I had befriended a young Puerto Rican mother from Massachusetts who was running from her abusive fiancé and her I became instant friends. She was smart beautiful had an infectious laugh and was wise beyond her years. She had 2 adorable daughters and was determined to create a safe and loving life for them. I lived with her for almost a year and learned so much about life and how to behave like a woman with wisdom and poise. To this day she remains one of my closest confidants and inspires me to continue to reach for my dreams. For her alone I'm thankful for the time I spent in the shelter. Shortly after my return to the shelter I ran into Carlzo again and 'rekindled' our grotesque romance but a couple weeks in he ended up giving me enough money to obtain my own apartment so I guess the tradeoff was worth it. I was so excited to finally have a place for my children to come home to again and I went to work putting together the cutest bedroom for them. It was decorated in crayons complete with red crayon bed posts for my daughter and blue crayon bed posts for my son. The walls had crayon wall stickers all over them and I was so excited and proud to show them that I was working hard on getting them back home and giving them the life they deserved. I went back to dancing occasionally but also picked up a job at a local restaurant and catering hall in order to make ends meet. It seemed like I was finally getting my life together at twenty years old. I had purchased a car, was off probation, in college, working part- time and visiting with my children regularly and looked forward to bringing them home.

Losing Alex

Spring of 1997. I had been officially separated for about 2 years when the divorce was finalized and had been living at my apartment for several months. By this point my ex-husband and I had established a Shared Parenting agreement with our now three yr. old son, with him as the Residential parent. I was granted visitation one week day evening and every weekend. The agreement was working out well as far as I could tell. I'd pick my son up Friday evening and drop him off Sunday afternoon. My daughter, a rambunctious ornery two year old, was only allowed to visit occasionally at my apartment, and since my parents had moved out of the Park by this point they made it clear I was not welcome in their new home despite my daughter living there. My lifestyle was too dangerous and unstable for them to allow me into their home they explained. I hated every second of not being able to visit with my daughter regularly was but since I had given them Temporarily Guardianship and was still working in the adult sex industry I believed them when they told me I would never be able to regain custody of her until I had my life completely together. I was so desperate that on several drunken occasions I would MapQuest their address, print out the paper and drive to their house in the middle of the night and just sit outside and cry feeling completely helpless on how to get my daughter back. I never dared knock for fear of losing vitamin all together. I would just sit there and stare at their house for hours while sobbing. One of my friends was also in a similar situation with her mother and daughter so we would concoct all these half ass plans on how we could make enough money to kidnap our daughters back and go on the run with them. We even began looking at wigs and disguises to pull this off but in the end we never ended up following through with our plans to kidnap our own children and resigned ourselves to the fact that we may not ever regain custody of our daughters again.

As a toddler, Alex maintained his cherub face with his pouty lips and amazingly long dark eyelashes with the sweetest demeanor of a child and was an absolute joy to be around. Despite what I was going through with visitation with my daughter, I knew that, no matter what I had a court order for my son and nobody was able to prevent me from visiting with him every weekend. So per the usual routine, on a Friday in March of 1998, I went to our previously designated location for pick up for our visit but after waiting about thirty minutes I began to realize Edward was not going to show up for the drop off. I tried to reach out to him by paging him and calling his house but got no response. I wasn't immediately alarmed since sometimes we had communication gaffs and tried not to think too much into it. We always managed to get any visitation issues resolved and back on track right away and so I went home assuming there was miscommunication and I would pick up my son the following Wednesday for our visit. .tut the following week I arrived at the drop off/pick up spot only to encounter the same scenario, no son and no correspondence from my ex-husband. Week after week I went to pick up my son to no avail while still getting no response from Edward. This went on for about a month or so until I became to demand answers from his mother. Initially she was no help at all stating she didn't know where he was and that she hadn't spoken to him she was no help at all. I finally began angrily demanding answers. And finally, during one particularly heated confrontation, when I furiously asked her "where the hell is my son?' She looked at me with shock and said "Oh, you really don't know? They moved to Georgia".

My world shattered right there in that moment.

Georgia? I was shocked sickened and devastated. How dare this man take MY child? After everything he did to me while I was still a child and now he takes my son? And how the hell was I going to get him back into the State of Ohio? I spent the weekend grilling his mother for information that she refused to give up and even dug through her trash hoping I could find a letter with a post mark from Edward, a phone bill with his number, ANYTHING that would direct me to the whereabouts of my son. That following Monday, I immediately headed downtown, straight to the clerk of courts to file contempt paperwork on Edward and have the judge order my son be brought back only to find out that a month earlier he had filed a motion for full custody and a petition to relocate. The problem was is that he high tailed it out of state before the court could serve me with paperwork and complete court proceedings. I approached the court seeking recourse for my son to be returned and was informed that I would need to file and mail contempt of court paperwork to Edward in order for a hearing to be granted to work through this. I filed charges immediately and mailed them to the address Edward listed in the court docket. Several weeks later I received a notice that my paperwork was returned as nobody by that name resided at that address. He only used that address for the court in order to relocate and never actually lived there. I had no idea where my son was or if I would ever see him again. And to top it off my ex-husband had remarried a woman named Lisa Jackson and she was with them as well.

I tracked down their marriage license from the courts and gathered all of the information I could on her and kept it tucked safely away in case I ever needed it.

The chase

I quickly developed some Private Investigating skills and utilized every tool at my disposal to locate my son. I knew the general area they were residing in, so I contacted the local Electric Company and concocted a story that secured me his address. I told them that I believed my ex-husband was using our child's Social Security number to fraudulently obtain utilities. The operator sounded shocked and eager to assist to I rattled off Edwards Social Security number pretending it was our child's. The lady responded sounding disgusted and quickly retrieved his address for me. Gotcha! I thought to myself. I then called the local library and had them run what's called a Criss Cross, a system that cross references the 4 closest neighbors to any specific address. I was giddy, after almost 4 months I had finally found my son! I contacted the neighbors with the information I was given only to find out that the family had moved out about 6 weeks prior and they didn't leave any forwarding information. I was back to square one. No address, no phone number, no son. Day after day I would spend my time thinking of ways to locate a viable address. My friends, sister and I would dig through his mother's dumpster searching for phone bills with out of state numbers on them and basically harass her asking where my child was, I put up missing child posters and raised money by placing coffee cans around the city in different locations with my child's picture on them, contacting the authorities in the area of Georgia I suspected them to be in only to be told that the case was Ohio jurisdiction and there wasn't anything they could do to help. About 3 years into this chase I was able to hire a licensed Private Investigation firm but after paying them a pretty substantial amount of money, they also came back amiss as they handed me a stack of addresses that I had already explored and cross referenced. My ex-husband was moving approximately every 3-6 months and every time I'd locate him he was long gone again.

It was the late 90's early 2000's and I was still bouncing around, living with friends and stripping. I would work at a bar for a bit get fired for doing something complete insane like urinating on other dancers outfits (she deserved it) or crawling back into the bar when it was closed in *an* attempt to rob it and whatever else my drunken mind could concoct. There wasn't a shortage of strip clubs to work at and the men, booze and the money were always plentiful, but it was starting to wear on me. There's only so many times you can lick your nipples before it just becomes another mundane boring act to arouse some pervert who's completely intolerable. There was the guy who liked for the heaviest girl with the longest stiletto to stand on him and dig their heel bearing their full body weight into his scrotum. He would sit there lying his head on the back of the couch moaning loudly in ecstasy as one girl after another would attempt to burst one or both of his testes by digging their heels into him, there were the leg patting old grandpas who would give you a dollar and a nice pat on your outer thigh every few minutes or the local drug dealers who would keep us stocked with cocaine but never wanted to pay more than two dollars for a dance, the regulars who you could always count on for a drink or few bucks, and the racists who would get drunk and not realize they were ranting about black people to a black woman. The married men who would take you back to their houses while their wives were out of town and the Mexicans, groups of Hispanic men who would travel the US doing asbestos abatement earning what would be today's equivalent of about $50 an hour. Some of them were from Mexico, some from Honduras, some from Guatemala and some from El Salvador. We just called them the Mexicans. They were big drinkers and even bigger spenders. They lived simply, all together in humble homes with little furniture and empty refrigerators. Large bags of Maseca filled the corners while the refrigerator housed large amounts of Roma tomatoes, jalapenos, cilantro, limes, onions and Corona beer. It was always stocked with plenty of Corona beer. Their ultimate goals were to save enough money to take care of their families back home as well as upon their return to their country never have to work again.

I stayed in contact with *Rosie* from my first club several years ago and we had become really good friends so I got her job at a club I was working at in North Akron. We were living together in a hotel up the street with her toddler son at the time and were trying to save enough money to rent our own apartment but it seemed the expenses from living in a hotel were allowing us to just break even. We were just stripping to survive at this point. We began to hang out with the 'Mexicans' and each of us picked our favorite. None of them were particularly attractive but they had money and we needed it. So she got her a cute little Honduran guy named Geno. I picked a Guatemalan dude named Louis who looked like the Quiznos sandwich creature and a New York sewer rat had a baby. He had a sharp pointy nose, straight jet black hair that grew over his forehead and was all around so unattractive to me. Money alcohol and drugs had me stooping to some pretty low levels. I was about 23 yrs. old at this time and he told me he was in his early 30's. About 3 months into the 'relationship' I found out he had purchased the identification card he was using and that Louis wasn't his real name. In fact they all had, none of their names were actually their names. Who knew who he really was? All I knew is that if I was going to keep myself out of the streets I was gonna have to pretend real hard to make this work. He was just so ugly and on top of that he wasn't circumcised and I had never encountered that before with a man. I wasn't sure if it was supposed to smell like that or what. I'll save you the gory details, just know that the odor made me gag before anything else had a chance to.

He would drink himself into oblivion for 2-3 days at a time. His head would wobble side to side like his neck couldn't support the weight of his big ugly ass head and face. After binge drinking for days he would become very aggressive and would get angry for whatever little infraction and start yelling while calling me names like "stoopid neeger beetch or " stoopid fooking beetch" before he would eventually just pass out. I would raid his wallet snatching hundreds and hundreds of dollars and take myself on shopping sprees at the local Village Discount. He'd wake up from his bender a day or 2 later angrily searching for his money. Every week I'd act surprised suggesting he lost it when he was drunk and this went on for months. Eventually the relationship became so toxic that he attempted to leave me stranded in Maryland while visiting his family. He and been drinking for 2 days straight by the time we left Akron and had been driving for around two hours when he began to become belligerent while yelling and swerving all over the road. I was terrified we were going to crash but he just kept yelling and swerving. Eventually he told me to hand him one of his Coronas he had in a cooler in the backseat. I climbed into the backseat, grabbed one and as I struggled to pop the cap I noticed a bottle of windshield washer fluid on the floor. I wasn't sure what exactly was in this stuff but I was hoping it was something that would get him sick so I opened the Corona and took a sip to make room. I quietly opened the bottle of windshield washer fluid and poured it into the Corona and it instantly turned the yellow beer to a bright green color. Well shit, I didn't think about that part happening and he was starting to wonder why I was taking so long and asking me "where's mai fooking beer beetch". I handed I to him and he looks at it and says "Whut dee fook ez thees". I blurted out the quickest thing I could think of and said it was one of the new Special Brew St Ides beers but he took a sip and spit it out all over the car. Great, now I'm trapped in a car with a raging mad drunk belligerent head wobbling Guatemalan who's telling me he's leaving me in Maryland when we get there. Luckily he sobered up at a family member's house and we headed back home to Akron two days later. As soon as we reached his house I packed all of my belongings, left and took the little money I had and got an apartment in North Akron. Rosa remained with her cute little Honduran for several years after this even moving out of state with him. She eventually gave birth to their son and moved back to Ohio where they lost contact. I never heard from Louis again.

Shortly after the relationship with Louis ended, I was situated and settled into my little apartment when I reconnected with an old male friend named Dale that I had met in the shelter several years earlier. I was about 4 years into the search for my son at this point and was still hitting dead end after dead end. It was a brief tumultuous and abusive fling and after only a couple months of hooking up before I ended up getting pregnant with my 3rd child. Dale was getting increasingly emotionally and physically abusive in the short time we were together and when I revealed my pregnancy to him he demanded that I get an abortion or he was going to 'give me one himself'. I was devastated and I wanted this baby more than anything in the world. This child would be my fresh start, and hopefully show my parents that I could be responsible enough to care for my oldest daughter as well. I was going to get my life together and show everyone that I wasn't this worthless piece of shit they all said I was. But he insisted that I was not going to carry this pregnancy to term so the following day I opened the phone book and sat there quietly sobbing and began looking for clinics. I called one and inquired about the pricing then hung up the phone and continued sobbing. I didn't want to do this, I wanted to keep my baby, this baby had given me hope that I could be a parent to at least one of my children and that it would fill the void in me.. I was 23 yrs. old with two children that I didn't have custody of and now another one on the way. With my limited education and only income coming in was from the strip club I wasn't able to maintain my apartment by the time I was in my second trimester and on top of the abuse he liked to cheat. By my end of my first trimester he had given me Chlamydia from his cheating and refused to leave when I was informed by my doctor that I had contracted and STD, so I decided to leave him in the apartment alone and move on with my life. Luckily by this time Rosa had secured and apartment in the Mohawk homes and I was able to move in with her. She had given birth to another baby by this point so it was her, her two children and myself tucked into this little apartment in East Akron. My oldest daughter was still with my adoptive parents and I was visiting with her very seldom since visitation was complicated by the fact that my parents still didn't welcome me into their home and were getting pretty tired of my inability to obtain stability. . I mean I get it, my lifestyle and choices were not something they wanted in their lives and they were taking care of my daughter, making sure she was loved and protected, and I really couldn't ask for more than that, but I still longed for my daughter to be with me. I just couldn't get a grip on getting it together long enough to give her the safe environment she deserved and that my parents required in order for me to get her back. I was still growing up myself and dealing with trauma that would manifest itself in many toxic ways over the coming years.

Rosa, her son and I lived together in her small apartment together while I applied for public housing and waited for my Section 8 certificate to obtain independent housing. Although I had stopped stripping, there were times when I would drink occasionally during my pregnancy, but for some reason I always seemed to want to commit felonies when I would drink excessively. And it wouldn't be anything light like wine or beer, I would go for heavy hard shit and it's a miracle that my daughter came out okay. I'd like to blame this portion of my decisions on my addiction, it might help me make sense of my actions, but it more likely immature childish decisions that was nothing more than pure neglect and abuse on my unborn child and it's a phenomenon that my baby came out unharmed. One drunken night, while about 6 months pregnant I devised a plan for Rosa and I to commit a burglary in our apartment complex. We had recruited a teenaged boy that was our neighbor to join our plot and waited until late at night to break into our neighbor's unit. She didn't have much of anything in there. She was a poor single mom in the projects just like us. But she owed Rosa money and was ignoring all our attempts at getting the money in question returned. Her electricity just so happened to be turned off the day we began to devise this plan so we knew she wouldn't be home when we went inside. As it got dark and we waited for our neighbors go head in for the night and for the complex to quiet down we continued drinking. Once it was nice and late and quiet the kid next-door went over to her windows with some tools and removed the screen that was attached by some type of screw. It took him quite some time to loosen all those screws then remove the screen and run it down to the dumpster. He let himself in through the window and opened the door for us. Victory! We walked thought the house in the dark with our flashlights while picking out our favorite items. I chose an old stereo system, a wooden wall shelf an 8x10 dirty area rug and an old Nintendo. There really wasn't much else to choose from considering the level of poverty we were all living in but with my housing voucher coming in soon I could use all this at my new apartment.

The next day before the neighbor could return to find her home burglarized I raced all the items over to another friend's house for safekeeping. When she came home that day she immediately walked over to our door with tears streaming down her face. We feigned shock and fake concern as we learned of the burglary and walked with her back to her apartment to survey the damage. After the police arrived we left and nervously watched them process the scene. They came and took statements from us then left. We took a sigh of relief thinking we had just got away with this and were mighty proud of ourselves. Two days later we as we sat in the living room a loud knock came at the door. It was the Detectives from the days prior. They stated they knew that we were responsible for the burglary and if we didn't return the items and confess they were going to take Rosa's son into custody and arrest us on burglary charges. I promptly went and picked up that old stereo, dirty rug, old Nintendo and wooden shelf and set the items on her back porch and ran back home. We ended up being charged with Receiving Stolen Property and were both placed on house arrest and given probation. My record was getting pretty lengthy but it still never dawned on me that the source of all my problems was alcohol. I didn't believe it was a problem since I was still an occasional binge drinker. I lived with Rosa for about 6 months before I obtained my Section 8 housing voucher late that fall and found a cute little duplex in Goodyear heights. I was eager to get moved in and set up since I was only a few months away from giving birth. Over those next few months of my pregnancy, I spent my time preparing for this new baby and creating a comfortable and safe home for her to live in. I cut out drinking completely and focused all my energy on working and creating the perfect little home complete with pastel pink nursery decorated in zoo animals while eagerly awaiting her arrival. My parents were excited for her arrival as well and we were finally getting along exceptionally well. I was visiting with my oldest daughter regularly on the weekends and we would make crafts, finger paint, watch TV and just hang out when we were together. I felt so relieved to finally be able to be a mother to my daughter and was hopeful for our future. Although I wasn't working at the time, I was able to maintain my home with a small welfare check until I gave birth and was able to secure a job. As I prepared for this new baby's arrival I still couldn't help but wonder when or if I was ever going to see my son again. Time just kept passing and he was nowhere to be found.

On a cold and blustery winter day in 2000 I began to feel the familiar pangs of labor. I was lying on my couch trying to fall asleep (since I didn't have a bed as of yet) when the pain kicked in. I called my mom to let her know that I was pretty sure I was in labor and she drove the forty minutes to my house to take me to the hospital. After 12 hours of a fairly easy labor and while the cold wind whipped through the trees outside, I gave birth to a beautiful seven pound absolutely perfect baby girl. For privacy purposes, this participant has requested to be referred to as Brown Lightning for the duration of this writing. She was angel of a little girl and came into the world with the sweetest demeanor and character for a child. As a baby, she rarely cried and although she could be a bit demanding when it came to eating she was overall a calm happy baby. But one thing we learned about her fairly early was not to piss her off because she would voice her displeasure by letting out the most ear piercing screeches. I mean this sound was so high pitched and would come from the pit of her stomach and she could go on angrily screeching for what felt like hours. She was a very happy well-adjusted baby who smiled all the time and my parents and I fell in love with her immediately. As her features developed she began to look just like me with very fair skin and super curly hair, almost like a mini-me and boy was she inquisitive and intelligent! She even began walking at 7 months old and would look like a little baby doll toddling around. This little girl seemed to be born wise beyond her years with the first words she ever spoke at 10 months old were "what is that". She had to know what EVERYTHING was and I would spend hours riding the bus with her explaining what each bush, house, car, cat, dog, telephone pole was. She would look out at the world with wide eyes and amazed at everything. She loved any and all animals, but kittens were (and still are) her favorite.

I wanted to do everything right with this baby. I made sure she had everything she could need and that our home was a warm and safe space for her. After her birth I began working at a local pizzeria and my mom would help babysit. I was breastfeeding at the time so I couldn't be too far away from her for too long so I only worked part time. My parents fell in love with her and her with them, and to this day they still share a very unique and special bond. I joined several parenting support groups and would have Help Me Grow workers that would come out and assist me with any parenting or life barriers I was experiencing She made it to every doctor appointment and wellness check and even took infant CPR classes after a scary incident on some stairs when she was 6 months old. I was hyper vigilant to ensure she was well taken care of and knew she was loved. With visitation with my oldest daughter on the weekends and working and taking care of an infant I was living a plain boring life and I loved every minute of it. I was hopeful that I would be able to regain custody of my oldest daughter in the near future and somehow find my son (who was now 7 years old) and bring him home as well. I felt more complete and hopeful then I had ever felt and my life appeared to be heading in the right direction, but then I began dating again.

A longtime male acquaintance would occasionally stop by for a visit with me and Brown Lightning. Over time he and I would begin building a sexual relationship with him, while he and my baby girl began to build the most adorable bond. As he would come by more and more frequently, he and Brown Lightning would play for hours while he played peek a boo with her and would make up the most ridiculous songs and she would just squeal with laughter. He used to get a kick out of the way she would stand up as a baby because it was truly the oddest thing any of us had ever seen a baby do up to that point .At any given moment she would be sitting with her legs out in front of her and just swipe her legs behind her and stand up. She didn't use her hands to push herself up she would simply just stand up. He would laugh and laugh saying he's never seen a baby do that before and to be honest I hadn't either, and still have never seen a baby do that. To this day my daughter still can go to a standing position with her legs straight out in front of her without using her hands.

He wasn't exactly what I was looking for in a man though. He was always bouncing around and never lived anywhere for too long, he would only work off and on and was covered in prison tattoos. He was loud and obnoxious and smoked pot like it was cigarettes but he never could seem to get high enough for his liking so he would just smoke blunt after blunt. I still didn't smoke weed any longer, as I was still traumatized by the odor from my time in the Rosemary projects. He idolized Tupac and would listen to every song by him on repeat for days on end I mean he was constantly rapping one 2 Pac song or another. He was also a talented and amazing writer and would write letters and poems to me and Brown Lightning all the time. Even though he wasn't was I was looking for or even a really good prospect, I began to look forward to him coming by over time we became intimate he moved in and voila! Instant family. He was extremely helpful with Brown lightning who consistently would come down with ear infections or break out in random bouts of hives. She always seemed to have some type of skin condition or fever going on and one time when she was finally sent home from the third Emergency room trip in as many days and was suffering a myriad of random symptoms, she was finally diagnosed with Scarlett Fever, It was shortly after her first birthday when this random illness occurred and Jeremy walked 2 miles in the middle of the night in a treacherous snow storm pick up her prescriptions so she could finally get some relief. He was an outstanding surrogate father and loved her deeply and I didn't mind as her biological father was continuing to be an abusive drunk. Within weeks of her birth I had already forbade him to see her unsupervised her due to the black eye he had given to his girlfriend at the time and I didn't want my baby around someone who was capable of doing that. On several occasions I would attempt to allow him visitation with her, but his behavior remained violent and aggressive so by her first birthday he was cut off permanently. Over the course of her life his behavior would improve temporarily then he'd be right back to being abusive to his current girlfriend or in jail or prison for domestic violence or stalking and I just didn't want my child subjected to someone who could behave in that manner. It was important that I kept this baby as safe as possible from harm.

Jeremy didn't have any children of his own and was always the life of the party when kids were around. He was full of life and goofy just like them and my girls were growing attached to him and even my parents seemed to like and accept him. We lived a pretty normal life at first and since we were both working part time, he would pitch in and help with Brown Lightning when my mom couldn't. I had managed to save enough to purchase a car but was still using a loaner van that my mom was letting me borrow so I wouldn't have to catch the bus with the baby. I eventually saved enough to purchase a car with the help of my dad, leaving me two cars at my disposal. Although Jeremy's driver's license was suspended, he assured me that he was working on obtaining valid license soon and from my observations he seemed to be a pretty safe driver. I really didn't mind letting him use my newly purchased car while he worked on getting his license situated until the day I pulled into my driveway and seen him walk out the door but there was no sign of my car. He had gotten pulled over for driving recklessly and my car was impounded. I was furious and forbade him to drive it anymore after I got it out of impound, but 2 weeks later, while the baby was with my mom and we were on a drunken bender he was driving the car around a bend and hit a curb too fast. I had been trying to tell him to slow down several times but he kept assuring me "I got this chill out". It was dark, the roads were covered in snow and I was terrified we were going to wreck. And that's exactly what happened, he hit a curve, hit the brakes and my white 1998 Pontiac Bonneville spun out in the snow several times before knocking down a telephone pole and finally resting on the curb. My car was totaled but we were alive and didn't need medical care and thankfully we walked away from it with some scratches and a bill for the pole because I told the police that I was the driver. I was getting pretty tired of the way he lived his life with reckless abandon because he seemed to have no regard for anything or anyone around him. Not in a malicious way just a very careless way. He would get aggressive if he didn't have his weed so most of his paychecks would be spent on that and whatever else was left was what he could contribute to the household. Sometimes it was only $20 and I would become irate. We had been together for about seven or eight months when I was beginning to realize that this man and relationship was not going to work out and I was finding myself becoming increasingly frustrated with his childish behaviors and all around irresponsibility, but before I could work up the nerve to end the relationship, our lives and home was rocked.

One cold February evening in 2002 I was contemplating on how to end the relationship while I was in the kitchen preparing dinner. I was making spaghetti with salad and garlic bread while Brown Lightning toddled around in the living room after just arriving home from a visit with her grandparents. We stood in the dining room talking as we heard what sounded like a freight train rumble through the small apartment. We stopped in our tracks and just stared at each other with our mouths agape wondering what the hell just happened. The house hadn't shaken at all and we didn't feel the ground rumble but there was a pretty intense storm going on outside so we wondered if we just had some type of tornado. We ran to the door to open it and survey the damage that surely had to be somewhere only to find out that the door wouldn't budge, it was blocked from the other side. We ran upstairs to my daughter's bedroom because it faced the front of the apartment only to find that there was a 30 foot tree coming through her bedroom window. The storm outside had uprooted the tree that was in the front of the property and the wind pushed it into our apartment that was situated in the back of the property and it landed promptly inside my daughter's bedroom. All you could see when you looked out was a wide open gaping hole where there used to be a wall. The entire top half of the tree and all of its branches were inside my house while the adjacent apartment building that sat across from ours didn't even have scratch on it. I was terrified and had no idea what to do so I called my dad (who had just dropped my daughter off) to come back immediate to pick her up, then contacted the Fire Department. My dad arrived faster than the AFD and I was able to hand my baby to him out of the back window and ensure her safety in case the tree fell further into the home. Several minutes later Emergency Services arrived and we also had to be rescued out of the back window as the front of the house was completely inaccessible due to the sheer size of the tree. We could only take what we could carry since the apartment was deemed inhabitable and an unsafe structure. The Red Cross was able to put us in a hotel for a couple days until we found more suitable permanent housing which was going to take months at minimum to locate another apartment/house and come up with the moving fees so I was stuck right back at square one. And since I didn't know where I was going to be living of course I couldn't take my infant child along with me until I figured it out so where did she end up? You got it, my parents' house. Luckily, after several days in the hotel a friend allowed us to use a spare room in her home until a room was available at the local Salvation Army shelter. It was a family shelter that provided single family apartments complete with full kitchen and bathrooms so I was able to have Brown Lightening stay there with me from time to time as well until I figured out how I was going to get out of this mess.

I had been living in the shelter for about 3 weeks when the pains began. Each day that passed my lower back was aching more and more and felt as though it was on fire to the point that I could barely walk. This is not the time or place for this to be happening I thought to myself so I would push through the pain because I absolutely had to locate suitable housing to continue working on getting all of my babies' home. By this time Jeremy had been placed in a Community Based Correctional Facility due to a probation violation and I was in the shelter pretty much alone. He would occasionally sneak over when he would receive a pass but that was few and far between and we would usually have just enough time for sex before he had to head back to the facility. Brown Lightning was there off and on but I didn't want her to grow up in a shelter so my parents often kept her. As the days progressed, and the pain intensified, I realized something was probably wrong so I finally called a taxi to the Emergency Department. I was expecting the doctors to tell me I had pulled a muscle or that my back was falling off my body and to send me home with some pain meds and directions to take it easy, but after several hours after arriving when they finally gave me my diagnosis, I immediately felt sick to my stomach.

Pregnant.

I couldn't believe what I was hearing. Jeremy had always told me that he was infertile and couldn't have children and since he was in his mid-twenties with no children I assumed it was true, although I had seen no medical documentation stating that was the case. Now here I was, homeless and pregnant with baby number four at the age of 25. With no education and on every government subsidy available, Section 8, food stamps, and Medicaid PIPP HEAP Christmas assistance, Easter assistance, Back to School assistance and food pantries. You name it, if it was free I was going to be in that line. I felt further away from getting custody back of my older two children than ever and no matter what I did I never could seem to catch a break. And to top it off this baby was already wreaking havoc on my body and I was in no position to parent another child. Jeremy was always in and out of jail and wasn't going to be a reliable parent, so I even though I wasn't ready, I had to get ready. And I was still searching for my son.

From the beginning, the pregnancy with this baby was unlike any other I'd experienced. On top of the stress from moving and dealing with Jeremy's constant stints in jail, the pregnancy itself was by far the most difficult. I was always having some intense random pain or just felt exhausted. Despite the obstacles I persevered and within a couple months was able to find a cute three bedroom house. It had two larger bedrooms just enough for the girls to have one to share and one for myself and the baby and the smaller bedroom I had set up for my oldest son. Although it had been almost five years since I had seen him at this point I was determined and vigilant so I set him up a bedroom and displayed the Birthday and Christmas gifts I had gathered for him over the years in a corner of the room. It didn't matter to me that an eight or nine year old child would come home to open toys suited for a five year old. Over the years I had purchased and gathered gifts for him for every occasion and I wanted him to know that he was loved and thought about every single one of those holidays.

As we settled into the new house and my belly grew, I began taking courses at a local Vocational School to obtain a General Office Clerical certificate. I deeply desired being able to better support my growing family and I knew I wouldn't be able to do that with the skills I currently possessed unless I went back to stripping. Even though I struggled with sitting through the classes while pregnant, I went each day and made a valiant effort to complete the courses before I gave birth. I found the classes valuable and was able to learn typing skills that have served me well to this day. As I got closer to my due date and we were adjusted and settled into our new home, I would earn extra money by babysitting so I could be at home with Brown Lightning and prepare for the baby. Jeremy had spent almost my entire pregnancy in prison from the violating his parole yet again. So I prepared alone while this pregnancy continued taking its toll on my body but as the end drew near everything came to a head when I was about 7 months pregnant. I was casually sitting on the couch watching television when out of nowhere I felt the most intense and sharpest pain that I'd ever felt in my rib cage. Almost like I had been stabbed and I wasn't sure if I was bleeding internally due to something rupturing or if something happened to the baby. I was rushed to the hospital by ambulance and raced to labor and delivery were they performed several tests to determine exactly what had happened. After all the examinations the only conclusion the Doctor could draw was that the baby had kicked me so intensely that he cracked my rib. I was under close monitoring from there on out and informed that if the pain didn't subside I would be placed on bed rest. Luckily, in the following weeks, the pain did subside enough that it was tolerable but I was still advised to stop attending classes and do as little as possible while the rib healed. After several more ob-gyn appointments to monitor the situation, the doctor decided that with the pain I was still experiencing, that I would be induced a few weeks before my due date to minimize the chances of any complications that might arise. I spent the following months searching for any information on my son while simultaneously researching Serial Killers. I became so enamored and fascinated by them and I would read any book I could get my hands on by Ann Rule or John Douglas and even began writing a couple serial killers in hopes they would correspond back so I could attempt to dig deeper into their mind and understand their thought process, but none of them ever did. This was before the internet and computers really became popular and I am not even sure how I was able to dig up so much information on these people in order to locate them or the Authors of these books but I was relentless in my pursuit of information. I had a real knack for coming up with creative ways to find out information and was becoming pretty inept at thinking outside the box. The years I spent hunting for my son I had to come up with unbelievably creative ways to track him down, and although I had tracked him down approximately four or five times at this point, my ex-husband was moving around so rapidly I always seemed to be just a step behind them.

Thanksgiving night of 2002, after spending a relaxing day with my daughters and parents, my mom drove me to the hospital and after fourteen hours and a normal labor and delivery I gave birth to my son. He was by far the easiest labor and birth out of all my children, since he seemed to just slide right out. This tiny black haired black eyed baby weighing in at six pounds and eighteen inches in length seemed to swim in the newborn clothes and he was the spitting image of his father. He was so little that I was actually scared to hold him at first because I was afraid I would break him, he was just so little. The Sunday after I gave birth, right before we were being discharged I got the usual three way call from the neighbor who facilitated the jail calls with Jeremy.

I hadn't spoken to him all week and he had no idea his son had been born, so when I relayed the news that his son was born he was elated. But his joy was short lived when I informed him that I had no plans on naming the child after him. We had been arguing my entire pregnancy about what we were going to name the baby since he wanted him to have his namesake, but by this point he had caused so much turmoil and chaos in my life that I truly didn't want the world to have 2 Jeremys. And since I had given birth without him present I had free reign over what to name this adorable little boy. So I decided to name him Cameron, though I did concede and gave him his father's middle and last name.

So here I was, parenting a toddler and a newborn yet again. Brown Lightening remained a sweet natured all around well behaved toddler with minor tantrums but my new beautiful bundle of joy was colicky fussy angry and all around frustrated with being born. Just like with my pregnancy, mothering this baby was a completely different and complicated experience. He hated to be swaddled, rocked or comforted in any way, so you'd have to hold him in an awkward position of cradling but not too tight and rock him side to side while he swung and punched at you until he finally passed out from fighting. He was about 2 weeks old and I was still working on perfecting my positioning to soothe this angry baby when he quickly arched his tiny body and just flopped right out of my arms. Thankfully we were sitting so he wasn't hurt but I realized from that moment on this was going to be unlike anything I had experienced before. Brown Lightning didn't care for this crying baby much and she would ignore him for the most part when she was home. Her and my parents bond was growing by the day and she absolutely loved to spend time at their house and being catered to day and night. Although my oldest daughter was still living there, it was becoming clear that Brown was emerging as the favorite grandchild. The relationship she built with my parents is something I have never seen them maintain with any of their children or other grandchildren. As Cameron got older and began to crawl and try to play with her she would climb into his playpen so he couldn't bother her. She would scream at him to get away from her and be all around mean any opportunity she saw fit and she didn't seem to care about the consequences of getting yelled at or placed in time out. She would just stare at me defiantly or ignore me when I would try to correct her. The stress was starting to wear me down as I attempted to manage an entire house for the first time and the extra expenses such as a water bill that came with it, raise children, work, and attend school while still trying to locate my son.

For a while I managed to keep it together and finished my certification n in General Office Clerical, but by the time I graduated the classes when my baby was four months old I was back working in the strip club. I had applied to a couple months prior but was turned away for being too overweight. I began taking diet pills and lost 25 lbs. rather quickly and went back for the position. I worked in a small family owned breakfast joint in the mornings and the club at night. For a while I held it together and even enrolled in college courses for Private Investigation which I was excited for. My mom would come over and babysit when I would work at the strip club and would spend the nights occasionally when I worked late. I remember one occasion I had come home so plastered that I felt the room spinning and like I was going to vomit. I held on to that vomit for dear life because I was so ashamed to have my mom hear me puking my guts up from being too drunk. She didn't really judge too much because she thought for the most part I was going to the club making money to support my family and coming home. She didn't realize that while I was at work I was using cocaine and would come home high as a kite trying to parent 2 toddlers. Some days I didn't even go to work. I would just have some random dude pick me up and go get high at his house for a couple hours. If you've never tried parent 2 small children, 1 with undiagnosed ADHD, while being high on cocaine for 2-3 days I would not recommend it. This has to be what hell feels like and to this day if I wake up before the birds and hear them begin chirping I panic for a split second and question if I have been to sleep yet. I probably have some type of PTSD from them birds honestly.

Jeremy was released from prison in the April of right after I graduated from Vocational School, when Cameron was just a couple months old. We attempted to reconcile and be a family, but shortly after his release he was back to his old tricks of not being able to hold down an job, smoking copious amounts of marijuana and when he didn't have any left he would become volatile and abusive so he ended up back in prison on a probation violation by September of that year. That summer I had begun taking classes for Private Investigation and I absolutely loved it. My teacher was a Homicide Detective with the Akron Police Department and since the class size was small and most of the time I would be the only one who showed up, she would relay stories of murderers she had caught. She had even worked on the Jeffrey Dahmer case, and since I had spent the last six months researching serial killers, I couldn't get enough of this class. I would even show up to class high off cocaine from the night before from time to time. I was enthralled.

Jeremy was released again and per usual we worked on reconciling yet again. He would help out with the kids and I would use the extra time to search for my oldest son and I needed all the help I could get because Cameron grew into a mischievous toddler and I would be completely overwhelmed with trying to figure out how to parent this child. He would come up with the most asinine ideas and I had no clue how to head him off, it seemed like every time I turned around this kid had found a more innovative way to cause chaos. He was pulling over dressers onto himself by the time he could walk, he would smear ketchup and mustard on the back porch to skate across and climb inside the oven and deep freezer. He would get so angry that he began banging his head on the ground, walls, whatever was flat nearby, he truly didn't care and once he actually banged his head on the concrete so hard that he chipped his front tooth. I would sit there scratching my head in bewilderment wondering when I should have taught him not to climb inside an oven. I mean, of course I explained to all of my children not to touch the hot stove. but I never ever had to tell them not to climb inside the oven. I was often left frustrated, exhausted and dumbfounded at his behavior. The weight of all this along with my son still missing, kick started an addiction with drugs and alcohol that would last almost a decade.

Fall of 2003, not long after Jeremy had been released again, he and I were going through the paperwork I had gathered the previous years on Isaiah. I was explaining to him how my ex-husband had remarried and that he had additional children with his wife and how I was bewildered that a whole family could continually move and seem to just drop off the face of the earth time and time again. She and Jeremy shared a common last name so I didn't think much of it when I discovered her maiden name through their marriage records several years earlier. There's probably millions of people in the United States with that last name, so the commonalty never registered. Then I revealed her name and his mouth dropped open and he just stared at me like he saw a ghost. He began asking more detailed questions about Lisa such as her parents' names and date of birth and he asked what her birthday was. I showed him all of the documents I had gathered with her name on them and he looked up at me, stared me dead in the eyes and said "That's my older sister".

To say I was I was dumfounded would be an understatement. To know that I've been dating the man whose sister has had my son with her all these years was mind blowing. But in a strange twist of fate, that also made my sons not only siblings, but cousins by marriage as well. Needless to say, I was ecstatic and the fire was lit with a renewed hope and fervor. The biggest obstacle was that Lisa was several years his senior and he hadn't laid eyes or spoken to her in almost a decade and had no idea where she was currently residing but he did let me know that she had always maintained regular contact with their father Phillip.

Once again I began asking family members if they knew where the family was residing and if anyone had any information on them. Phillip didn't know much about where or how they were living outside of the general area of Georgia they were living in, nor did he have any way to contact them as Lisa would only contact him intermittently throughout the years and it was usually for money. Phillip also didn't believe that she was in contact with any other family members who would know their whereabouts. It was beginning to feel like another dead end. How could I keep getting so close but still be so far away? It had been five years now with no contact with my child and it seemed like no matter what I did I was always a step or two behind them. I figured I'd try asking his mother one more time if she knew where her son was hiding my child and after an intense shouting match where she became exasperated and extremely frustrated she accidently blurted out "I don't know what room they're in!!" She had no idea but in that moment she told me everything I needed to know about where my child was and I knew exactly how to find him. My son was living in a motel.

Why else would she say room? Reasonable deduction led to believe that It would be extended stay as they had children with them and would need to be able to store and cook food. I called every extended stay motel in the 20 mile radius of the area I was told they were residing in. On July 7th 2003, after making about 8 or 9 calls, the front desk clerk of a Super 8 motel in Georgia answered the phone and I nonchalantly asked to be transferred to Edward Morgan's room. My heart felt like it immediately seized in my chest when she said "hold please". Was this really the same Edward Morgan I had been hunting down for the last several years? I waited with baited breath to be transferred and when I heard the ringing on the other line I panicked. What would I say? I knew I couldn't confront him and let him know I discovered his hideout because I couldn't risk him running with my child again. After three rings a low raspy voice that I knew all too well answered the phone and said "Hello".

It was Edward, I'd know that voice anywhere. So I sat there quietly holding my breath not daring to make a peep as to not give away my identity and listening to the background noise hoping to hear just a snippet of a child's voice before I ended the call. But unfortunately I heard nothing. I wanted to do nothing more than to scream and cuss him out and tell him how much I absolutely hated him and to bring my child back home immediately, but instead I hung up without saying a word and sat on my couch sobbing uncontrollably in complete shock trying to register what just happened and kept replaying the last five and a half years of searching, fighting, crying and praying over and over in my mind. I had finally did it, finally found my son and all I needed to do now was get an address and have him served. I called the front desk clerk back and asked if the guests are able to receive mail there, she informed me that they didn't but that most of the long term guests use a P.O. Box located across the street inside of a Mailbox Plus store. I called the store and confirmed that Edward Morgan did in fact have a P.O. Box registered there and they supplied me with the number on it. That night I cried myself to sleep. I couldn't believe it was finally over and now all I had to do was get my ex-husband served and this nightmare could end. I actually did it. Despite all the obstacles, abuse and trauma I had endured I fulfilled my promise to my son that he would never ever wonder why he wasn't 'enough' for his mother to fight for him.

After 1.951 days, almost five and a half years of sheer hell, I had finally found my son.

And so it begins………

The tumultuous trauma ridden, yet victorious story of a young girl born out of wedlock to a young interracial couple in Akron, Ohio, in the late 1970's. Tamara's biological mother had no plans on becoming a young single parent, but with no assistance from the child's father and very little education, she had no means to support her child. Eventually the young mom and had to make the unthinkable decision of relinquishing custody and giving her only child up for adoption at the tender age of three years old, leaving Tamara to be adopted into and raised in a Caucasian household.

Perhaps this story is how Tamara survived a childhood, where the trauma of her adoption left her searching for a place in this world to belong and call home, with a family of her own, or perhaps it's a story that accounts for her survival. From enduring abuse and neglect from birth, to trying to fit into a world where she never truly felt like she belonged, Tamara spent the majority of her life searching for herself and a place to belong while simultaneously piecing together the tattered shards of her family.

Tamara endures poverty, homelessness, teenage motherhood, sexual assault, that culminated in an addiction that ravaged her family over the course of 2 decades.

This story embodies resilience, never allowing your circumstances to dictate your outcome while learning from your mistakes, and most of all, the power of a mothers love.